AMERICAN
WOODWORKER™

WOODWORKING
TECHNIQUES

Rodale Press, Emmaus, Pennsylvania

Printed in the United States of American on recycled paper containing a high percentage of de-inked fiber.

Library of Congress Cataloging-in-Publication Data

American woodworker woodworking techniques.

    Includes index.
    1. Woodwork.   I. Rodale Press.
TT180.A4   1988   684'.08   88-4370

ISBN 0-87857-770-X   paperback

2 4 6 8 10 9 7 5 3 1 paperback

Contents

Sawing & Grading Wood

By Christian Becksvoort

METHODS OF CUTTING

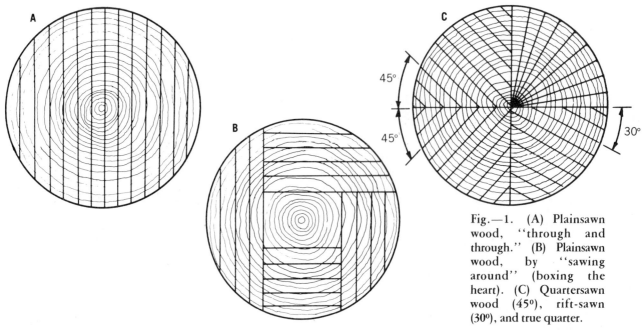

Fig.—1. (A) Plainsawn wood, "through and through." (B) Plainsawn wood, by "sawing around" (boxing the heart). (C) Quartersawn wood (45°), rift-sawn (30°), and true quarter.

There are two general methods of sawing lumber, plainsawn or flat-sawn, and quartersawn or rift-sawn (figure 1). Plainsawn wood is by far the cheaper, more common, and more readily available. Some sawmills will not even attempt to quartersaw.

Plainsawn (in hardwood) or flat-sawn (in softwood), as the name suggests, is a relatively simple method by which the log is passed through the blade in the same position until it is completely sawn into boards. A variation, called sawing around, involved cutting until defects are encountered, then turning the log 90°. Plainsawing is cheapest and most efficient because it involves very little rotation of the log during the cutting process and leaves very little waste. By definition, flat-sawing means that the angle of the growth rings is between 0° and 45° to the wide surface of the board. This results in the wide-figure patterns seen on the faces of plainsawn lumber (figure 2). To some, this pattern is much more attractive than quartersawn wood. Knots, when present, are round or oval; thus the board is stronger than a quartersawn board (which usually has spike knots across the entire face of the board). Plainsawn wood is less likely to collapse in the kiln and shrinks and swells less in thickness.

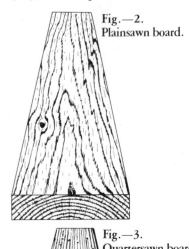

Fig.—2. Plainsawn board.

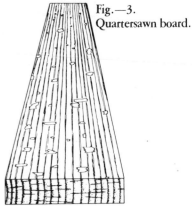

Fig.—3. Quartersawn board.

Quartersawn (in hardwoods) or vertical - or edge-sawn (in softwoods) is a little more complex. The log is first sawn in half, longitudinally, then each half is again sawn in half, resulting in four equal quarters (see figure 1). These are then tipped on their points (the pith or center of the log) and sawn in one of several ways. Most commonly, the quarter is just sawn through and through, with the blade at 45° to the two flat edges of the quarter and all saw cuts parallel to each other. An older and more difficult method is to set one flat edge of the quarter almost parallel to the blade and then cut a series of thin, pie-shaped boards. This involves repositioning the log after each cut so that the blade passes through the point of the quarter each time. Old clapboards were almost always sawn this way. Rift-sawing, a variation of quartersawing, means that the flat sides of the quarter pass at 30° and 60° to the saw blade. True quartersawn wood has the growth rings at an angle of 60° to 90° to the wide face of the board. Rift-sawn wood has the growth rings running 30° to 60° to the wide face. Quartersawn wood lacks the large figure pattern of plainsawn wood. Instead, it shows a series of parallel lines, the edges of the growth rings. Species with conspicuous and long rays, such as oak, form a beautiful fleck pattern. The biggest advantage of quartersawn wood is that there is almost no cupping or twisting and only a minimum of shrinking and swelling across its width. There is usually less surface checking, and raised grain caused by ring separation is less pronounced. In use it wears more evenly and holds paint and finishes better, depending on the species. Sapwood is confined to one edge of the board, and is limited to the width of the sapwood in the log.

A close look at the plainsawn lumber in figure 1 shows that if the wood is sawn through and through, a few boards next to as well as above and below the pith will be quartersawn, since the sawblade passes almost directly through the center of the log at this point.

When to use quartersawn or plainsawn wood? Quartersawn is preferred under circumstances in which warp, shrinkage, and expansion must be kept to a minimum and when wear is an important factor. For example, quartersawn wood is preferred in floors where the boards are subject to wear and must remain flat, and where the gaps between them must be kept as small as possible. Quartersawn wood is also ideal for clapboards, where warping, shrinkage, and expansion must be minimized, as well as for door frames, any frame construction, and unsupported shelves or breadboards. On the other hand, when the appearance of the wide, flowing figure of plainsawn wood is desired and the wood is properly restrained to prevent warpage, plainsawn wood is the proper choice. For panels in frames, case sides, drawer fronts, and even tabletops, as long as the wood is given room to move (as in a frame and panel) and supported to prevent warping (as in a dovetailed corner), plainsawn wood is fine.

Since plainsawn lumber is much cheaper, more common, and easier to find, quartersawn wood cannot always be used where it best suits. Out of necessity, any available lumber must therefore be substituted. Allowances must be made to provide for shrinkage and expansion.

GRADING LUMBER

Hardwood is graded into three categories, depending on its use and market: finished market products, dimension parts, and factory grades. Finished market products are cut and graded at the mill in their finished form; there is little or no remanufacturing involved. These products include flooring (by far the largest volume), siding, ties, lath, construction boards, trim, molding, stair treads, and risers. Both dimension parts and factory grades are intended for remanufacture. The difference is that dimension parts are graded on overall clarity, while factory grades reflect the proportion of a piece that can be cut into useful smaller pieces. Factory-graded lumber is most commonly available at lumberyards and is also sold to furniture manufacturers. Consequently, the grading for this type of lumber is the most important for the woodworker. Rules for grading are those established by the National Hardwood Lumber Association. The grades, from best to worst follow: Firsts and Seconds (FAS), Selects (Sel), Number 1 Common, Number 2 Common, Number 3A Common, and Number 3B Common. The standards for each grade are quite complex and include allowable minimum width and length, and the number of cuttings allowed per board to produce a given percentage of clear wood. For example, FAS has a minimum allowable width of 6 inches (15 cm) and a minimum length of 8 feet (2.4 m). The board can be cut up to three times, depending on the length, and must yield 91⅔ percent clear wood, with a minimum cutting size. On the other hand, Number 3B Common lumber has a minimum width of 3 inches (7.5 cm) and a minimum length of 4 feet (1.2 m). The board can be cut an unlimited number of times to produce a clarity of only 25 percent. Defects taken into consideration when counting the number of cuttings include knots, checks, wane, bark, rot, and insect damage. Sapwood is not considered a defect. A complete listing of standards for each grade is shown in figure 5.

The grading of softwood is a different story. There are nine or more private organizations, each of which sets standards for one or more species of softwoods. For example, both the Northeastern Lumber Manufacturers Association, Inc., and the Northern Hardwood and Pine Manufacturers Association set standards for white pine. In general, softwood lumber is divided into construction lumber and lumber for remanufacture.

Construction lumber consists of stress-graded, nonstress-graded, and appearance lumber. Stress-graded lumber is 2 inches (5 cm) and thicker, and is graded not to appearance but for strength. It is used for studs, joists, posts, beams, and stringers. Nonstress-graded lumber is used for siding, shelving, paneling, and subflooring. Grades in this category are No. 1, No. 2, No. 3. Appearance lumber is graded for appearance only, not structural integrity. Graded B and Better, C and Better, and D, it is used for finish work, trim, flooring, ceiling, casing, and built-in cabinet work.

Lumber for remanufacture is composed of several categories, each with its own rules and standards. These include factory or shop grades, industrial clears, structural laminations, and various other standards for molding, ladders, tank, pole, and pencil stock.

For the small-woodlot owner who uses his own stock, these rules are of no real consequence. To anyone cutting and sawing for resale, however, as well as the woodworker purchasing wood from a mill or lumberyard, the rules covering the specific wood type should be known and understood.

About The Author
Christian Becksvoort is a cabinetmaker and a contributing editor to **The American Woodworker.**

This article excerpted from the book **In Harmony With Wood.** *Copyright 1983 by Christian Becksvoort. Used by permission of Van Nostrand Reinhold Co., Inc.*

Fig.—5. Standard Hardwood Cutting Grades[1]

Grade and lengths allowed (feet)	Widths allowed	Surface measure of pieces	Amount of each piece that must work into clear-face cuttings	Maximum cuttings allowed	Minimum size of cuttings required
	In.	Sq. ft.	%	Number	
Firsts:[2] 8 to 16 (will admit 30 percent of 8- to 11-foot, ½ of which may be 8- and 9-foot.)	6+	4 to 9	91⅔	1	4 inches by 5 feet, or 3 inches by 7 feet
		10 to 14	91⅔	2	
		15+	91⅔	3	
Seconds:[2] 8 to 16 (will admit 30 percent of 8- to 11-foot, ½ of which may be 8- and 9-foot).	6+	4 and 5	83⅓	1	Do.
		6 and 7	83⅓	1	
		6 and 7	91⅔	2	
		8 to 11	83⅓	2	
		8 to 11	91⅔	3	
		12 to 15	83½	3	
		12 to 15	91⅔	4	
		16+	83⅓	4	
Selects: 6 to 16 (will admit 30 percent of 6- to 11-foot, 1/6 of which may be 6- and 7-foot).	4+	2 and 3	91⅔	1	Do.
		4+	see[3]		
No. 1 Common: 4 to 16 (will admit 10 percent of 4- to 7-foot, ½ of which may be 4- and 5-foot).	3+	1	100	0	4 inches by 2 feet, or 3 inches by 3 feet
		2	75	1	
		3 and 4	66⅔	1	
		3 and 4	75	2	
		5 to 7	66⅔	2	
		5 to 7	75	3	
		8 to 10	66⅔	3	
		11 to 13	66⅔	4	
		14+	66⅔	5	
No. 2 Common: 4 to 16 (will admit 30 percent of 4- to 7-foot, ⅓ of which may be 4- and 5-foot).	3+	1	66⅔	1	3 inches by 2 feet
		2 and 3	50	1	
		2 and 3	66⅔	2	
		4 and 5	50	2	
		4 and 5	66⅔	3	
		6 and 7	50	3	
		6 and 7	66⅔	4	
		8 and 9	50	4	
		10 and 11	50	5	
		12 and 13	50	6	
		14+	50	7	
No. 3A Common: 4 to 16 (will admit 50 percent of 4- to 7-foot, ½ of which may be 4- and 5-foot).	3+	1+	[4]33⅓	see[5]	Do.
No. 3B Common: 4 to 16 (will admit 50 percent of 4- to 7-foot, ½ of which may be 4- and 5-foot).	3+	1+	[6]25	see[5]	1½ inches by 2 feet

[1]Inspection to be made on the poorer side of the piece, except in Selects.

[2]Firsts and Seconds are combined as 1 grade (FAS). The percentage of Firsts required in the combined grade varies from 20 to 40 percent, depending on the species.

[3]Same as Seconds with reverse side of board not below No. 1 Common or reverse side of cuttings sound.

[4]This grade also admits pieces that grade not below No. 2 Common on the good face and have the reverse face sound.

[5]Unlimited.

[6]The cuttings must be sound; clear face not required.

SOURCE: U.S. Forest Products Laboratory, *Wood Handbook*.

Compensating For Movement

By Christian Becksvoort

Gluing Panels

The days of single plank table tops are gone forever. And so, after a piece has passed the planning stage, panels must be glued up. A panel is nothing more than a series of boards of the correct length glued together edgewise to give the correct width. Stock should be cut to the required length, with enough boards to make up the width, allowing enough for jointing. Grain and color should be matched to give the appearance of continuous grain across the entire surface. When gluing panels one must choose which side of the board faces up. If all boards are quartersawn, this presents no problem — either side will do. However, plainsawn lumber (with its wide, wavy pattern) has a tendency to warp; all conditions being equal, the growth rings have a tendency to cup away from the center of the tree. Therefore, most texts will recommend that the growth rings be alternated; one board up, one board down. Then, as the individual boards in the panel cup, the worst that can result is a wavy panel. Gluing together all boards with the rings running in the **same** direction will result in an eventual cup much more pronounced than the small waves of the previous method. But, assuming that both panels will be used as tabletops, the more pertinent question may well be: which panel is easier to keep **flat**? To keep the small waves in panel 1 flat, almost every board in that panel would have to be screwed down; whereas only one or two screws would be sufficient to hold down Panel 2 (figure 1). What is more important is that by placing all growth rings in the same direction, with the older wood (that which grows toward the center of the tree) **up**, any sapwood can be left on the board and be put under the table. This saves quite a bit of wood, especially in cherry and walnut or wherever the appearance of sapwood is not desirable.

Jointing boards is a quick process with a power jointer or, after a little practice, with a long hand plane. A crisp, clean butt joint is all that is necessary for optimum strength in panels. Fancy tongue and groove joints are used in industry so that boards can be aligned by machine, but add no more to the strength of the joint. Doweled joints are not worth the effort either; again, they help to align the members but add little, if anything, in strength. Moreover, since the dowels are inserted at right angles to the boards, this can result in crossgrain gluing if glue finds its way into the holes, and can actually lead to cracking along that joint. The hole itself has only two small areas of long-face grain, the rest being end grain and contributing to a weak joint. This explains why dowels are not advisable in tables or chairs as replacements for mortise and tenon joints, which are much stronger.

Some texts also recommend leaving a 1/64-inch (.35-cm) gap at the center of two boards about to be glued, but this technique is recommended only when the boards are expected to shrink further. The assumption here is that clamps will close the gap until the glue dries (which they do), and then as the boards dry the ends will shrink across the grain, relieving the pressure at the center. As noted previously, moisture exchange between wood and air occurs most rapidly at the ends of the boards. Now suppose that the panel is glued up in a heated shop in the middle of winter when no further possible shrinkage is likely to occur. The center of the boards, under pressure when clamped, is likely to undergo additional pressure as the ends of the boards take up moisture and expand; this can lead to splits near those glue joints. The moral here is to use the moisture meter in the center **and** the ends of the boards (especially after a long or severe humidity change) before leaving any kind of a gap. Anticipation of future humidity conditions can go a long way in preventing checks and splits.

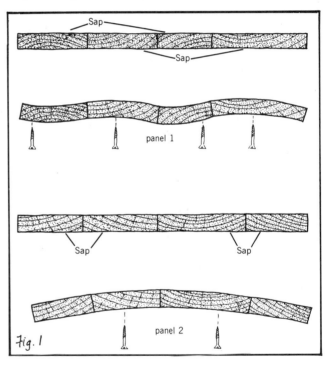

Alternating growth rings result in a wavy top, while boards glued with the rings running in the same direction form one gentle cup, easier to hold down with fewer screws.

"The days of single plank table tops are gone forever..."

GRAIN DIRECTION IN CASES

Bureaus, kitchen cabinets, cupboards, desks, stereo cabinets, dressers, blanket boxes, and display cases are all considered "case goods." Whether any of the six sides are open is not important. The outer box, without its various drawers or doors, is called the carcass. From the cabinetmaker's point of view, one of the primary considerations in constructing the carcass is which way to run the grain around it. By maximizing the amount of grain running in one direction or plane, cross-grain construction is minimized. That leaves only two or three choices, as figure 2 indicates. The most common method in case construction is to have the grain run up one side, across the top to the other side, and down to the bottom (A). With this method the carcass expands from the front to the back, while its height and width remain constant. This front-to-back movement ensures that

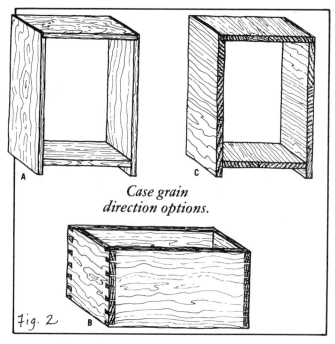

Case grain direction options.

Fig. 2

the size of the front remains the same, making drawers and doors easier to fit. The second method (B) is usually most suitable in blanket box construction. Here the grain runs around the left side, front, right side, and back, like a belt. This means the top and bottom remain the same size, but the box itself gets taller or shorter as the seasons change. That creates no problems, since there are no doors or drawers to fit. The lid, however, is another matter, since it shrinks and expands in width, especially as it is usually hinged in the back; all the mvoement will therefore be most apparent in the front. The third option is to have the grain run front to back on both sides and the top, which aesthetically and structurally is the most unsatisfactory (C).

CASE CONSTRUCTION

Once the grain direction has been decided and the panels glued, the actual building process can begin. Sand both sides and the top, joint one edge, and cut to width. Cut sides, perfectly square, to height, and the top to length. Select the best sides of all three panels and mark as the outsides. Next, rabbet or groove the back edges to accept the back. Depending on the type of joint used on the top and

whether or not a molding is to be used, the rabbet in the top may have to be stopped. Now cut the joint used to fit the top to the two sides. This could be a screwed butt joint, a single or double rabbet joint, dovetails, or a splined miter. A little planning is in order for the next step, since it is now time to make the dadoes and grooves for any interior dividers, shelves, doors, or drawers; it is much easier to accomplish this **before** the pieces are glued. Now the top can be screwed, glued, or clamped to the sides. A temporary spacer will keep the bottom of the sides parallel. While the glue is drying, you can construct the bottom and any dividers. If solid shelves, dividers, and bottoms are used, this presents no problem, since they will slide into the dadoes and the grain will be in the same direction as the top and sides, assuring that all movement will be front to back. In some instances drawer dividers are merely frames that allow the drawer to slide in and out, yet save a considerable amount in weight and raw material (figure 3). These frames, however, will not move in the same manner a solid divider would, since the sides of the frames run at 90° to the grain of the case sides. Because of this potential movement, frames cannot be glued into place, but are best attached by nailing. The case is turned upside down, and the frames slid into the dadoes, starting at the top (which is the bottom dado, now that the case is upside down). Finishing nails are driven at a slight diagonal through the frame and into the case side. They must not show underneath the frame or on the outside of the case side. Two or three nails will suffice to hold the frame in place, yet will allow the sides to move. Nailing across the grain is allowable, since the nails permit movement of the wood. Figure 4 shows the basic steps in case assembly.

This process is continued until all frames are in place. The last one, the bottom, should be solid wood if it is to house an open compartment. If it is merely the last drawer frame, then it must be constructed with grooves and floating dust panels. If desired, all frames can have dust panels.

Squaring the case prior to attaching the back is most important. Place the carcass face down either on the floor or on sawhorses. Assuming that both sides were cut to the same length and the top and bottom of the case are the same width, a potentially square box exists. Measure from the top left corner to the bottom right, and from the top right corner to the bottom left. These measurements should be identical. If they are not, a clamp can be used to pull the longer of the two opposing corners into position. The carcass is now ready to accept the back.

In solid wood construction, backs are usually loosely fitted individual boards, rather than one solid glued-up panel. By using smaller individual pieces, the total shrinkage and expansion of the back will be distributed across the entire width, rather than at both sides of the back, as each board is allowed to move independently. One of three commonly used joints can be chosen to allow movement yet exclude dust and light from the case: spline, ship lap, or tongue and groove (figure 5). Under no circumstances should any of these joints be glued; they **must** remain loose in order for the back to move. The choice of joints is not totally arbitrary. If the back is to be made of expensive primary wood (if it is an open case or if glass doors are used), then a spline is called for, since up to ½ inch (1.25 cm) is lost in overlap on the tongue and groove and ship lap. If the back is to be thinner (on a small display case or desk), then a ship lap is less subject to breakage during assembly than either an extremely thin tongue or spline. Tongue and groove joints can be used on thicker backs.

In determining the amount of gap to leave between the individual boards, common sense and a moisture meter are both helpful. Kiln-dried wood used in the middle of January will expand in a few months, so leave a bigger gap. Wood at 14% M.C. used in July can usually be butted tightly. Now nail the back across the top and all dividers, and down both sides with finishing nails. It is good practice to countersink the nails.

Turn the case over and recheck for squareness. It is now ready for face strips or a full front frame to cover the drawer dividers. The face strips are made of primary wood, dovetailed into both sides, and glued to the secondary wood dividers. No problems here, even though two different woods are glued, since the grains run in the same direction.

glued its full length, since the top and any face frame are running side to side also.

Another alternative is not to add molding, but rather to shape a molding pattern directly into the front and two sides of the top (figure 7). The top must be wider and longer than the case to allow for the overhang and can be attached with screws and cleats. This works especially well on blanket box tops. Trying to apply molding to three sides of a single board top (or panel) is chancy at best; molding must be anchored along both sides (which are end grain), and neither nails, glue, nor screws can hold it. The "integrated molding" is much easier to construct, and movement ceases to be a problem.

MOLDING

The case can now be sanded and is ready for any molding that needs to be applied. In applying the molding, a difficult situation is encountered. A top molding must be flush to the surface, remain tight at the miter, remain the same width as the case, and be strong enough to serve as an occasional handle to lift and move the case. Obviously, a small piece of wood attached across the grain of a case cannot meet all these requirements at the same time. A look at almost any piece of antique case work will attest to that. All too often, glue is used in the vain hope of stopping the inevitable movement of the case side. Molding on antique furniture was almost always applied with finishing nails. This served the purpose, but just barely: while the molding was held in place and the nails did allow movement, the mitered corner opened and closed at the whim of the weather, and eventually the molding worked itself loose. A slight improvement over this method is to glue the mitered joint and the first inch of molding, use finishing nails on the rest of the length, and then sink a screw as close to the miter as possible. This can be done from the inside, if there is room to work, or directly into the molding. A plug cut from the waste material of the miter can be used to fill the hole (figure 6). With this method a small amount of glue and a screw keep the miter closed year-round, the finishing nails allow for movement, and all the expansion and contraction of the case side is limited to the back — a compromise at best, but one that works well. The front molding can of course be

Case assembly procedure: (A) After top is attached to sides, turn case upside down, and nail drawer frames into place from below. (B) Square the case to adjust a-c to equal b-d. (C) Nail back into place. (D) Apply face frame, either a partial frame (top half) or full frame (bottom half). (E) Case is ready for sanding on all surfaces. (F) Apply moldings. Construct and fit doors and drawers.

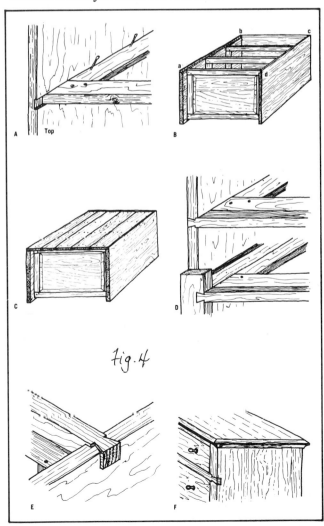

Drawer divider construction and cross section showing dust panels.

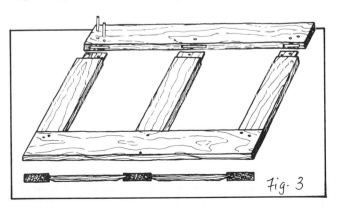

Fig. 3

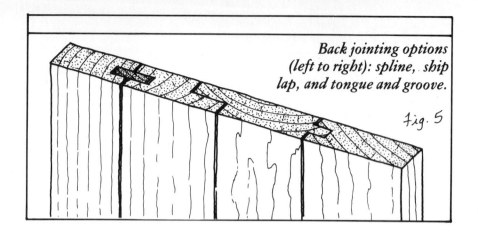

Back jointing options (left to right): spline, ship lap, and tongue and groove.

fig. 5

This article excerpted from the book In Harmony With Wood. Copyright 1983 by Christian Becksvoort. Used by permission of Van Nostrand Reinhold Co., Inc.

fig. 6

Molding can be screwed and plugged at miter.

fig. 7

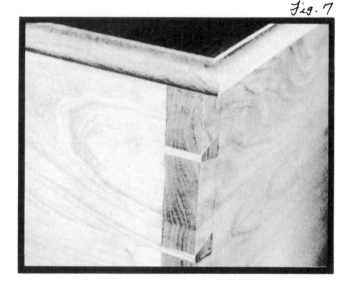

Molding shaped directly into top.

WOOD DOES MOVE IN FUNNY WAYS

Even the casual observer will notice that something has happened to this piece, causing a change to occur between each end. The change, of course, was caused by the draftsman's pen and not to be confused with the movement of wood.

(Editor's Note): I am sure that there are many of you who have seen this drawing before, but we could not resist presenting it one more time. If by chance there is a beginning woodworker out there somewhere who has not had the opportunity to try to make one of these, try at least once. If you succeed, please send me a sample. I have been trying more years than I have gray hairs, but all I have to show for my effort is more (or less) gray hairs.

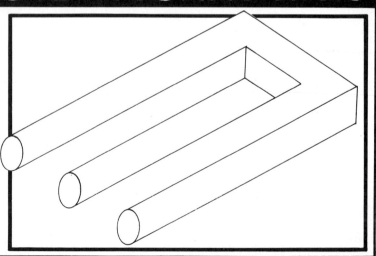

Carcase Construction

By Franklin H. Gottshall

Cabinet making, furniture building and design may be roughly divided into two categories. One of these consists of furniture with open framework, such as beds, tables, and chairs. Pieces belonging to this category have little or no enclosed areas. Easily distinguishable from the above is carcase furniture, which has partially or wholly enclosed areas, designed and constructed in such a manner as to enable one to store goods. Chests, chests of drawers, and cupboards are included in this category. Cupboards, when fitted with glazed doors even serve as display cases as well as storage coffers.

Carcase work, in furniture design and construction, consists of a "box". In its most elementary form, such a box will have six sides, like the chest shown in figure 1, consisting of a front, a back, two ends, a bottom, and a top or lid. When these six sides are joined together, as shown in figures 1, 2, 3, 4, 5, and 6, they form an enclosed storage area, and one of the simplest forms of carcase construction to be found in furniture design.

The six pieces may be joined together in a number of other different ways, the dovetail joint shown in figure 1 being but one of these. Front, back, ends, and floor could be held together with nails or wood screws, as is the floor in figures 4 and 5. Tongue-and-groove joints, easily formed on a table saw, may be used. In figures 6 and 6-A tongue-and-groove joints are used to join sides, ends, and bottom. The method of holding the bottom in place, shown in figure 6, is superior to the way it is done in figures 4 and 5. No glue need be used if this method is used, but some provision must be made to allow for swelling and shrinking of a board as wide as the bottom, and this has been indicated in the note on the right of figure 6.

Many other kinds of carcase construction have evolved from the basic box type represented by the six-board chest. Other chest types evolved from a desire to increase storage area and to vary the appearance in order to distinguish one example from another. This resulted in establishing types and period styles.

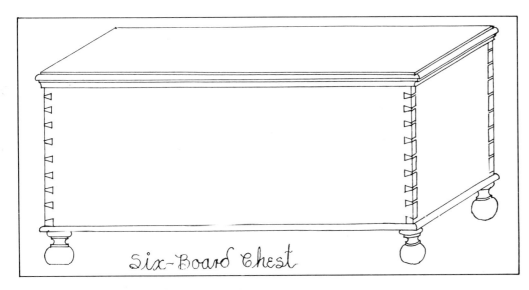

Six-Board Chest

Figure 1

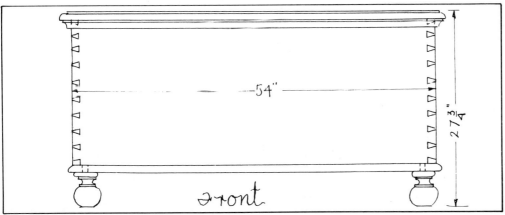

54"

27 3/4"

front

Figure 2

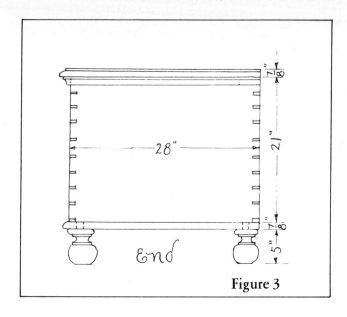

Figure 3

Areas were paneled, carved, painted, inlaid, and otherwise embellished. Legs were added as part of framework, and these were extended below the chest making it possible to add one or more shelves near the floor. By adding rails, stiles, panels, doors, and drawers, still more goods could be stored.

*W*ith the establishment of industry, and improvement in the social status of individuals during the middle ages, craftsmanship improved, and many new forms of furniture evolved. Cupboards, chests of drawers, wardrobe and other compartmented combinations evolved. The Small Bedroom Dresser shown in figures 7 and 8 shows such a piece of furniture. It has two drawers, and a cupboard below. Chests, while they can be made to hold a great deal, confront one with the necessity of having to remove a considerable amount of what they contain in order to find what is stored near the bottom. This undesirable feature can be greatly improved by substituting closets with shelves, or with still shallower compartments such as drawers.

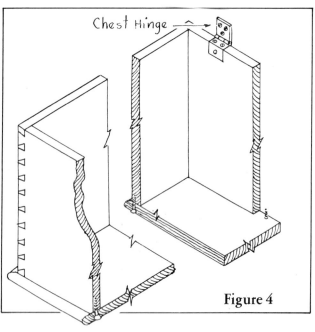

Figure 4

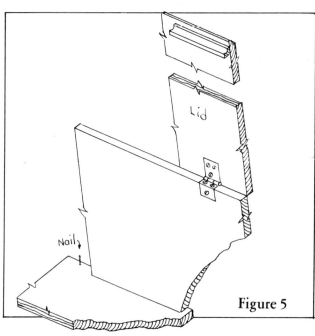

Figure 5

Construction Details

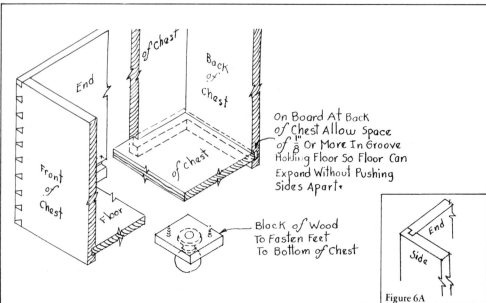

On Board At Back of Chest Allow Space of $\frac{1}{8}$" Or More In Groove Holding Floor So Floor Can Expand Without Pushing Sides Apart.

Block of Wood To Fasten Feet To Bottom of Chest

Figure 6

Figure 6A

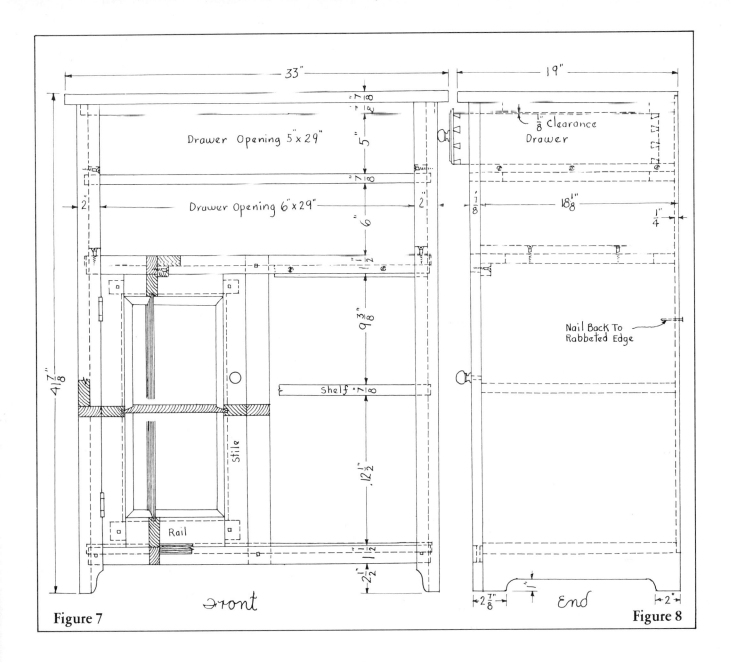

Figure 7

Figure 8

he doors in figure 7 are paneled, and these panels are held in place in sturdy frames. Mortise-and-tenon joints holding the frames together are glued and reinforced with wooden pegs driven through the joints. Panel edges are recessed into grooves, deep enough on vertical stiles to permit some expansion in panel width when season changes call for this. Since panels will not shrink nor swell vertically, no extra groove depth need be provided in top and bottom rails.

Floors should be sturdy, and firmly held in place on such pieces of furniture. Figure 9 shows how this is done by cutting grooves across both ends to support the floor. The floor may be glued to both ends, but need not be, since mortise-and-tenon joints holding rails and stiles together above and below the doors, securely hold the ends and floor in place at the front. When the plywood back is nailed to ends, top, and floor and to the frames which support the drawers, sound, sturdy construction is achieved.

The floor surface should be raised at least ¼'' above the bottom rail to provide a door stop when doors are closed, as shown in figure 9. Sturdy frames should be made to support drawers, and also as a base to which the top may be fastened. The rails comprising these frames should be joined together with mortise-and-tenon joints, as shown in figure 9. Dovetails on both ends of the front rail on the top frame fasten it securely to both ends of the carcase.

Figures 10 and 11 show a Slant Top Desk which has a compartmented interior in its supper section. The storage area in the desk's lower section is a chest of drawers. The drawers are supported on sturdy frames and the ends of these frames are recessed into the ends of the desk to hold them securely in place, as shown in figure 12. The bottom frame is fitted with plywood dust panels. While some furniture designers advocate putting dust panels under all drawers, I never considered this necessary, or even desirable. It has been my experience that instead of keeping dust out these additional dust panels collect more dust than they keep out. Dust panels in the bottom frame give sufficient protection, and an occasional cleaning job under the bottom drawer is a desirable precaution.

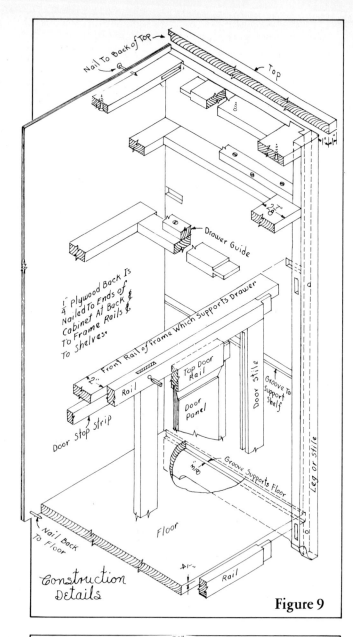

Nail To Back of Top

Top

1" 1"

2" 7"
8

Drawer Guide

1" Plywood Back Is
4 Nailed To Ends of
Cabinet At Back &
To Frame Rails &
To Shelves.

2" Front Rail of Frame Which Supports Drawer

Rail

Top Door Rail

Door Stile

Groove To Support Shelf

Door Panel

Door Stop Strip

Leg or Stile

1"
16

Groove Supports Floor

Floor

Nail Back To Floor

1"
4

Rail

Construction Details

Figure 9

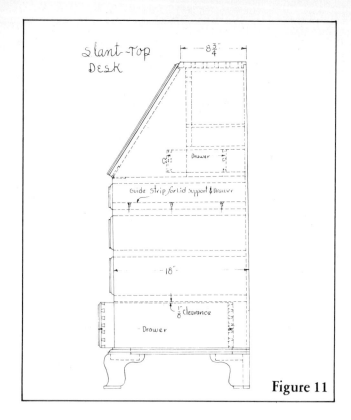

Slant-Top Desk

8 3/4

Drawer

Guide Strip for Lid Support & Drawer

18"

1" clearance
8

Drawer

Figure 11

*M*any old desks of this kind have the compartmented section inside the upper storage and work area built in by recessing shelves into both ends of the desk. I find this type of construction awkward and more difficult than the method shown in fig. 13, where the inside cabinet is made and put together as a separate unit, and then put into place before the top and the plywood back are permanently installed.

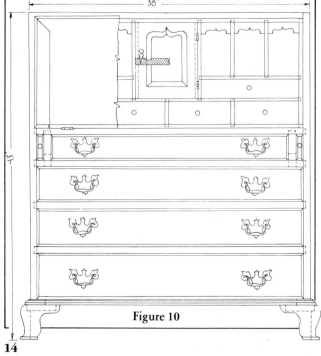

38"

43

Figure 10

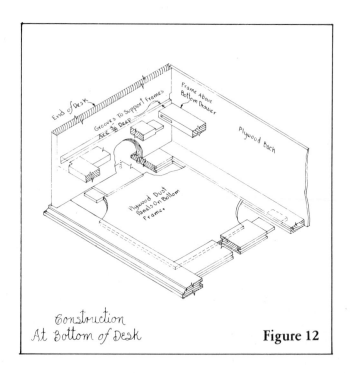

End of Desk

Frame Above Bottom Drawer

Grooves To Support Frames
Are 3/8 Deep

Plywood Back

Plywood Dust Panels On Bottom Frame.

Construction At Bottom of Desk

Figure 12

14

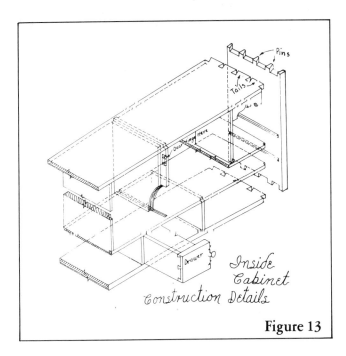

Inside Cabinet Construction Details

Figure 13

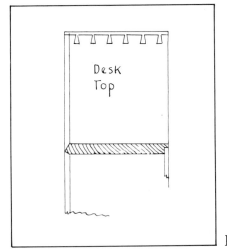

Desk Top

Figure 14

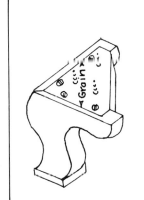

Shows How Foot Is Made & Fastened To Bottom Frame

Figure 15

Partitions on this inside cabinet are thin, and thus require careful fitting to do a good job. Upright partitions, and shelves are carefully fitted into grooves, and these grooves are made first, so that ends of shelves and partitions can be planed and sanded to exact thicknesses to fit into the grooves. One should not try to adjust groove widths to the thickness of the material going into them, but should always make the grooves first and then fit shelves and partitions to go into the grooves.

The top of the desk is dovetailed to the ends of the desk, as shown in figure 14. This kind of joining serves the double purpose of holding the upper part of the main frame securely together, and is also an indication of beauty and quality. Drawer sides, fronts, and backs are also put together with dovetail joints. It should be observed that pins on good looking dovetail joints are noticeably narrower than tails, as shown in figures 13 and 14. This desirable feature is seldom found in machine-made dovetail joints, but can easily be achieved when the greater part of this work is done with hand tools. Figure 15 shows how feet are made, and fastened to the bottom frame under the desk.

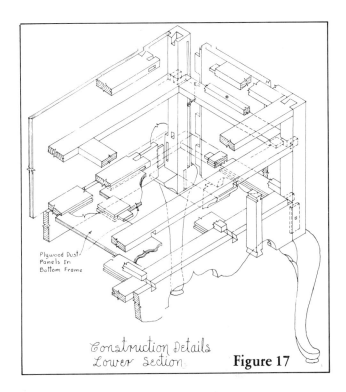

Plywood Dust Panels In Bottom Frame

Construction Details Lower Section

Figure 17

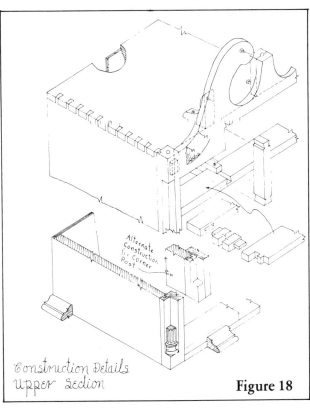

Alternate Construction In Corner Post

Construction Details Upper Section

Figure 18

*T*he Queen Anne Highboy, shown in figure 16 is an example of two carcases combined to make an impressive piece of furniture. The highboy shows a low chest of drawers supported on four legs, beautifully formed, and with another larger chest of drawers superimposed upon it. The relatively great height, the beautifully formed top and bottom, all serve to make such an item a desirable piece of furniture in any home.

The frame which supports the three small drawers in the lower section, is fitted with plywood dust panels, as was the bottom frame in the slant top desk. None of the frames above it need dust panels, since all drawers remain closed most of the time, and this feature in the bottom frame adequately provides the protection needed. Front and back rails of the upper frame in the lower section are joined to the tops of all four legs with dovetail joints, which securely holds this part of the carcase together. The glued and pinned mortise-and-tenon joints at both ends of the bottom rail in front, and the plywood back, when nailed to legs and frames in the rear, serve the same purpose there.

Dovetailing the top board to both ends of the highboy at the top results in the sturdiness needed there.

A notation about drawer construction is worthwhile here. Dovetail joints like those advocated throughout this article impact quality and sturdiness. The drawer fronts on the highboy have a lip extending about a quarter of an inch beyond the drawer opening on three sides — on upper edge and both ends. This lip on the drawer fronts is the shape of a quarter-round molding and its purpose is to close cracks around the drawer as the result of clearance needed at top and at drawer sides to keep the drawers from binding as they are being pulled out or pushed in. On most pieces of furniture, drawer clearance should be about 1/8'' to keep them free from binding. The quarter-round shape is cut on the bottom edge of the drawer front, as well as on the extended edges, but it cannot be extended here. If it were, the danger of breaking it off when the drawer is removed from the chest is too great.

Queen Anne Highboy

Figure 16

Discovering New Techniques

by Rhett Zoll

In the construction of my drawing table I developed two techniques that I would like to share with other woodworkers. The first is a split frame and panel system that I had to incorporate into the table after it was glued up, and the second is a ratchet system which is more versatile.

After gluing up my drawing table, which included four legs, aprons and a stretcher frame, I realized the table had too much movement from side to side. The frame and panel was the best solution both structurally and aesthetically. This included a panel with a top and a bottom rail with the legs serving as the stiles. The method allowed me to glue the pieces in without having to disassemble joints or force pieces together.

I marked on the legs the exact location of the rails and mortises. The mortises were connected with a ¼ x ¼ groove for the panel to slip into (see Figure 1). Next, I cut four floating tenons and glued them into the mortises (see Figure 2). I then measured the distance between the back legs, at both top and bottom locations for the rails.

Top elevated to display long leg of ratchet system. A drawer for paper drops down from front, suspended by two leather straps.

Then I prepared the rail stock and cut it to rough length. Each piece was resawn and planed to 3/8'' which cleaned up the band-saw marks. Clamping the halves together as though they were still one piece, I cut a ¼ x ¼ groove in one edge of each piece for the panel to rest in. I then cut the rails to their exact lengths. Since the legs are curved, the shoulders had to be cut at compound angles that related to the compound angles of the legs. I laid out and cut mortises in both ends of each rail that corresponded to the floating tenons glued into the legs. I cut the ¼'' plywood to length to allow ¼'' to enter into each leg. The plywood was then veneered with cherry and sanded. After all sanding was done, I began the glue-up.

I glued the bottom rail halves around their tenons, then sprung the plywood panel into the grooves. The top rail halves were glued and set around their tenons and everything was clamped up and allowed to dry.

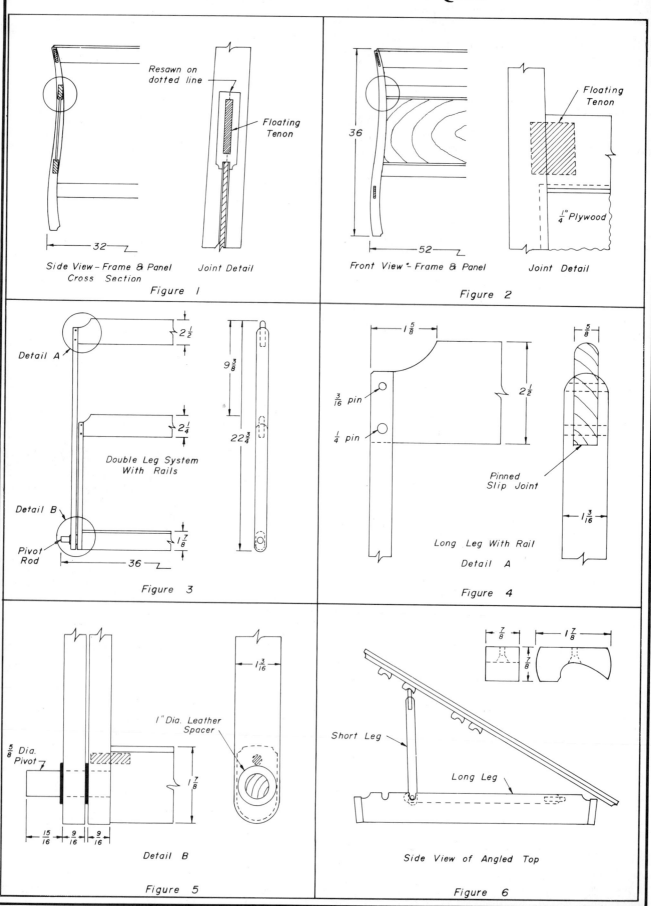

Resawn on dotted line

Floating Tenon

36

32

Side View – Frame & Panel Cross Section

Joint Detail

Figure 1

Floating Tenon

$\frac{1}{4}$" Plywood

52

Front View – Frame & Panel

Joint Detail

Figure 2

Detail A

$2\frac{1}{2}$

$2\frac{1}{4}$

$9\frac{3}{8}$

$22\frac{3}{4}$

Double Leg System With Rails

Detail B

Pivot Rod

$1\frac{7}{8}$

36

Figure 3

$1\frac{5}{8}$

$\frac{5}{8}$

$\frac{3}{16}$ pin

$\frac{1}{4}$ pin

$2\frac{1}{2}$

Pinned Slip Joint

$1\frac{3}{16}$

Long Leg With Rail

Detail A

Figure 4

$1\frac{3}{16}$

$\frac{5}{8}$ Dia. Pivot

1" Dia. Leather Spacer

$1\frac{7}{8}$

$\frac{15}{16}$ $\frac{9}{16}$ $\frac{9}{16}$

Detail B

Figure 5

$\frac{7}{8}$ $1\frac{7}{8}$

$\frac{7}{8}$

Short Leg

Long Leg

Side View of Angled Top

Figure 6

Drawing by Frank Pittman

Front view of drawing table with frame and panel construction across back legs. It is made entirely of cherry. (Drawing surface dimensions are 63'' x 40½'')

The pivoting rods fit into either of two sets of notches cut into the base. This allowed for further variation in changing the angle of the drawing surface. The top of the legs, which are connected by rails (see Figures 3 & 4) fit into one of four sets of individual notches mounted under the drawing surface.

This system worked extremely well throughout and has taken out all of the side movement. Visually, the frame and panel unifies the piece and serves very well as a modesty panel.

There were three criteria required of the ratchet system; a low and high angle for the drawing surface, nothing to hang above or below the apron, and a drawer to be contained within the same section as the ratchet system.

The ratchet consisted of six parts: four legs of two different heights, and three rails of three different lengths. The bottom rail, which serves as a pivoting bar, was turned on the lathe to produce the rods on each end (see Figures 3 & 5). The legs have a hole ¾'' from the bottom of each which fit snugly over the rods. The short legs, inside set, are glued and pinned with a ¼'' dowel to the pivoting bar, leaving the long set free. As one set supports the top, the other set lays flat inside the table (see Figure 6).

To keep the legs from rubbing together, or rubbing against the base, I fastened leather spacers on each side of the long leg set, which fit around the pivoting rods (see Figure 3 & 5, shaded area).

Back view showing frame and panel and short leg of ratchet system.

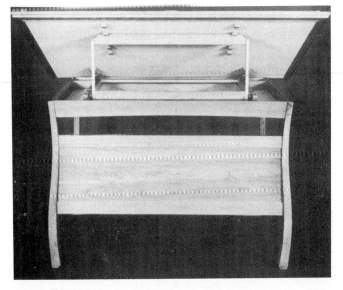

Detail of ratchet system in both supporting and relaxing positions.

With the double leg system, two sets of notches on the base and four sets of notches under the top, I am able to position the top at sixteen different angles, which adds much versatility, giving me a low angle of 22º and a high angle of 65º.

(Photographs by Frank Olma.)

ABOUT THE AUTHOR:

Rhett Zoll is a senior at Indiana University of Pennsylvania with a concentration in woodworking and furniture design.

Improving The Quality of Routed Edges

By Walter J. Morrison

The ideal routed edge is one that faithfully reproduces the contour of the router bit while requiring a minimum of additional work after it comes off the router.

The need for touch-up sanding, removing wood-fuzz from the work due to cutter dullness, or the repair of chipped-out stock after routing are examples of additional work one might encounter if care is not exercised during the routing process. By following a few basic practices however, the home woodworker can keep these problems to a minimum, resulting in an improvement in the finished quality of edges produced in the home shop. The practices detailed below will give you a better insight into the art of routing. Putting them into practice will give you better results.

- **WORK PIECE PRESSURE.** Don't unduly force the workpiece against the router bit guide. All this does is dent the workpiece.

Exerting too great a contact pressure between the router bit guide and the workpiece will result in an indented and burnished area on the routed edge. Avoid this by getting a feel for the required cutting pressure on a scrap piece of the same species of wood before routing the workpiece. As an additional safeguard against denting or burnishing the stock, a piece of masking tape can be applied over the area of the edge where the router bit *guide* makes contact with the workpiece. This will help to prevent denting as well as reduce the amount of burnishing of the edge due to the router bit guide post. Remember to cover only the area of the edge where the guide post makes contact and *not* the area where cutting is to be done.

Using the right pressure also extends router bit life. Excess cutting pressure causes high friction and can overheat the router bit. A sure sign of this is a bluish discoloration of the metal post on non-ballbearing type router bits. Those with ballbearing guides do not have the friction problem, of course.

To correct a dented or burnished edge requires sanding of the contour with a medium grit paper in the direction of the wood grain until smooth.

- **CUT IN COMPLETE PASSES .** Before cutting, "dry run" the router over the work to avoid any unplanned obstacles.

It is important to make each cut of the edge to be routed in a complete pass from end-to-end. If, for some reason, the tool is allowed to stop along the edge, the cutting load on the router bit is reduced, thus allowing the cutter to speed up.

This can result in a different surface finish from the rest of the edge in the area where the tool was stopped because the cutter is burnishing the wood instead of cutting it. This may become apparent only later when staining the workpiece. The burnished area is likely to resist staining, resulting in a light spot in the finished piece. *(If this cannot be avoided, the burnished area should be carefully sanded in the direction of the grain with a medium grit paper to break down the burnished surface.)* Another problem that arises from stopping the cutter on the surface is the creation of a "welt" or ridge on the routed surface where the tool motion was stopped. This is caused by a difference in the contact pressure between the tool and the workpiece before the welt and after the welt. *(If this cannot be avoided, carefully pass the router over this area in the direction opposite the original cutting direction. This should remove the ridge. Repeat as necessary.)*

To avoid these pitfalls in achieving a smoothly cut edge, "dry-run" the router over the edge to be cut with the workpiece clamped as it will be when the true cut is taken. In other words, with the router power switch turned *off*, pass the router over the edge exactly as the cut is to be made. This preliminary step will verify that no obstacles are in the way for achieving a complete cut in one pass. Such things as the router power cord being too short, the cord getting caught on a clamp or the workbench itself, or you, yourself, not having ample room to maneuver the router smoothly are examples of obstacles that will give you all of the welts and ridges you can handle. By doing a "dry-run" you can make sure all of these things have been eliminated.

- **VIBRATION FREE CLAMPING.** The better clamped the workpiece, the less chance of chatter and splintering.

The workpiece can easily be made to vibrate with the energy applied by the router if the workpiece and router are not kept in firm contact with one another. To avoid this, make sure, when using your router mounted on a router table, that you hold the workpiece firmly against the router bit with the bottom face of the workpiece flat against the work table. When using the router "free-hand", make sure the workpiece is securely clamped to a sturdy bench and is not free to move. Make sure that it is clamped so that it does not rock. In addition, grip the router with both hands, keeping it in positive contact with the workpiece throughout the entire cut. By doing these things you can minimize the ridges and splintering that can result on the routed edge if the workpiece is free to vibrate.

• RATE OF TRAVEL. The slower the rate of travel the cleaner the cut.

High speed router bits cut away stock in chip form, each cutter successively biting into the workpiece. Ideally, a good job occurs when the rate of travel is slow enough to allow each cutter ample travel time to overlap the cut of the previous cutter, thus providing a smooth transition between the action of individual cutters. If the rate of travel is too fast, this overlap is reduced and the edge begins to get rougher. To reduce the chances of this, try different rates-of travel on different wood species with your router. Through experiences, establish a rate of travel that produces a finish you are satisfied with. Remember that the optimum rate of travel is one that allows the machine ample time to cut away the desired stock cleanly and one that is physically comfortable for you. Remember, the slower the rate of travel, the cleaner the cut you will generally achieve.

• CUT 3 / FINISH 1. Route each edge in a succession of cuts. Make three cuts at increasing depths *against* the direction of the cutter with the last cut set to the final depth. Then make one more cut at the same depth setting but in the *same* direction as the cutter to finish. (See Fig. 1.)

Removing stock with a router bit is best done in a succession of cuts of increasing depth. This prevents the router and the bit from being overloaded as can be the case when a full-depth edge cut is attempted in one pass. Trying to remove too much stock in one cut can lead to uneven cuts and chipping of the finished edge, not to mention the likelihood of burning the router bit due to excessive load. Instead, if the job is spread over three cutting passes, the router being adjusted for a deeper cut each time, the resulting edge will be smoother and your tools will last longer. As an extra finishing touch, run the finished edge past the router one more time at the same depth setting as the last cut. Only this time, run it in the same direction as the cutter rotation. This will clean up any slight imperfections from the previous cutting passes. Try this technique on scraps first. For varying species of wood you may want to increase the number of cutting passes due to wood hardness, the amount of detail that the router bit has, and the power of the router.

• DON'T ASK FOR TROUBLE. Some miscellaneous hints for a better job.

1. When routing edges that have been sawn into curved or decorative shapes, make sure that the edge has been sanded smooth of saw marks, etc., before routing. Otherwise, the guide post on the router bit will dip into each imperfection, "telegraphing" the defect into the routed edge.

2. Never turn the router on or off while the work is in contact with the bit. This is unsafe, not to mention the damage that can occur to the workpiece. Always allow the router to achieve full speed before cutting.

3. Always make contact between the router bit and the starting point of the workpiece slowly to avoid chipping the work. Always break contact between the router bit and the end of the workpiece slowly to avoid having the bit roll around the routed edge and begin cutting the trailing end of the workpiece.

• SAFETY CONSIDERATIONS

1. Wear appropriate eye protection while routing. The router is a high speed device with a lot of stored energy. *[Ed. Note: Safety glasses without side shields are **not** adequate.]*

2. Always keep a firm grip on the workpiece when using a router/table combination and a firm grip on the router when doing "freehand" work. Always keep your eyes on the area being cut. Keep your hands and fingers a safe distance from this area by using the proper guides and clamps.

3. When turning the router off after completing a cut, allow it to completely stop before setting it down or reaching into the bit area.

4. Have work on a table that is of a comfortable working height for yourself.

5. Keep the work area free of obstacles that can snag your clothing or catch a power cord, etc.

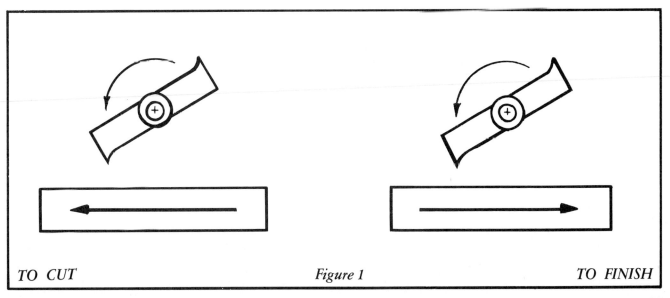

TO CUT   Figure 1   TO FINISH

The Wedged Through Tenon

By W. Curtis Johnson

Through tenon joints that are wedged are easy for the beginner because the use of the wedge compensates for minor errors. It is a particularly strong joint for joining the end of one board to the interior of another. The end grain of the tenon provides a decorative feature and the joint can be accented with a wedge of contrasting color if that fits with the design. If you have been reading James Krenov's books on woodworking, you have probably noticed that this fine craftsman uses the wedged through tenon in some of his furniture.

The key to a perfect mortise and tenon joint is to cut the more difficult mortise first, cut the tenon slightly oversize, and then trim the tenon to fit. Trim to fit is a method that allows working wood to a thousandth of an inch in many cases. The most notable exceptions are dovetails and box joints which should be sawed correctly the first time.

Mark out the mortise with a knife and an adjustable square (Fig. 1). The board should be flat and smooth with the edges and ends square so the mortises can be marked accurately on both sides. Size the width of the mortise about 1/64 of an inch less than the thickness of the board with the tenon to allow for trimming. The length of the mortise is a matter of personal choice, but since there is no gluing strength between the end grain of the mortise and the tenon, it shouldn't be too long. I am using 1¼ inches here with a ¾ inch board. If the board you are joining is wide, you will need more than one mortise and tenon.

The gauge line cut by the knife will provide a positive reference for cutting the sides of your mortise. Deepen the gauge lines a bit with your knife being careful not to widen them too much. If you cut from each corner toward the center you will avoid cutting past the corners. Now use your chisel to take out

FIGURE 2. Deepen the gauge line and remove a chip to define the edge of the mortise.

a chip from the inside of the mortise. Do this all along the gauge line (Fig. 2). If your chisel isn't sharp enough to shave with, sharpen it first. Now you have positive, square sides for the edges of your mortise where they are most important. Use your drill to remove as much waste wood as is practical from the center of the mortise. Try not to get closer than 1/32 of an inch to the gauge line.

Choose a chisel that is about 1/8 inch narrower than the width of the mortise to remove the remaining wood from the sides. Again, be sure the chisel is sharp. The pocket formed by removing the chips will allow you to hold the chisel vertically and in the correct position. Tap the chisel with a mallet, but don't cut too deeply. Remove the waste as you proceed by taking out chips with the chisel. After you have cut half way through the board, turn it over and cut from the other side. When the bulk of the

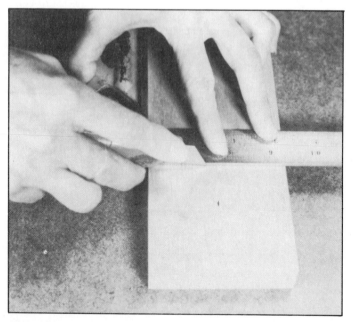

FIGURE 1. Cut the mortise first. Mark a gauge line by scoring with a sharp knife and an adjustable square. Do this on both sides of the board.

FIGURE 3. *Use a chisel and a mallet to remove the waste that remains in the mortise after drilling out the center. The pocket formed by removing the chip will help to place the chisel and keep it vertical.*

FIGURE 5. *The wedge will be inserted in a kerf sawed diagonally across the tenon. The wedge will tighten the tenon in the mortise compensating for minor errors.*

waste has been removed, sharpen your chisel once again and use it to square and smooth the sides of the mortise. It won't matter if the end grain is slightly undercut since there is no glue strength here. However, sides should be carefully squared. Widen the mortise if necessary. You can compensate when you cut the tenon (Fig. 3).

With the mortise completed you are ready to cut the tenon. It should be about 1/64 of an inch longer than the thickness of the board with the mortise. Score around the end of the board with a marking gauge or a knife and square to define this length. Mark the width as 1/64 of an inch wider than the mortise. I now simply cut the tenon with my bandsaw, but it can be easily cut by hand (Fig. 4). Score and remove a chip from the waste at the gauge line as you did for the mortise. With the pocket it is easy to saw on the waste side of the gauge line with a fine dovetail saw. A table saw or a radial arm saw could also be used, but be sure to use the proper jigs to make it a safe procedure.

The next operation is to fit the tenon to the mortise. The Record 073 rabbet plane is made to do this job, but you can do it just as well with a scraper if the tenon is only slightly oversize. Smooth the faces first, starting at the gauge line. When the corners of the tenon fit in this dimension, smooth the edges until the tenon fits snugly. You will have to tilt the scraper quite far to get into the corners. Alternatively, you can trim the tenon on a bandsaw.

If your tenon fits perfectly you may wish to glue it without the wedge. However, the wedge will add strength as well as hide imperfections at the viewing surface. The trick here is to wedge on the diagonal so as to tighten all four surfaces at the same time. Saw a wedge with an angle of about 4 degrees

(1/8 of an inch over 2 inches) (Fig. 5). The grain of the wedge should run parallel to the grain of the tenon. Tap the wedge into the kerf and carefully shape it to the tenon. Next try the wedge with the tenon in the mortise to ensure that you have about ¼ inch to drive in after gluing.

When all is ready, put glue in the kerf and on the surfaces of the mortise and tenon. Assemble the joint and tap the wedge carefully into the kerf. It need not be too tight, so don't overdo it. After the glue is dry, plane or sand the joint smooth, and admire your handiwork.

FIGURE 4. *The tenon can be cut on a band saw or by hand. Cut it slightly oversize and then trim to fit the mortise.*

ABOUT THE AUTHOR: *W. Curtis Johnson is an amateur woodworker living in Corvallis, Oregon.*

How To Lay Out and Make Dovetail Joints

By Franklin H. Gottshall

Dovetail joints are an essential and important part of fine cabinetmaking. In figure 1 a method for determining the angle of dovetails is pictured. This angle of about ten degrees is not an arbitrary angle, and slight variations will be found on furniture pieces, as well as on antiques you may see. The sliding T-bevel can be set to this angle to draw the dovetail angles; this step is being done in figure 3.

Figure 2 shows the first step in making layouts for dovetail joints. Since tail members vary greatly in width and since dividing the spaces equally is a desirable requirement, figure 2 illustrates a practical method of going about it. Because dovetail joints are made on boards of various widths and because these widths are not always easily divided into the number of tails and pins needed, lay a ruler across the board at an angle, which permits you to divide the width of the board into the number of equal spaces needed. These spaces are not necessarily an inch apart; spacing units can be any convenient size.

Because my sliding T-bevel square is fairly large, I find the protractor shown in figure 13 easier to use than the T-bevel for setting the angle. My protractor has a blade adjustable to any angle, which makes it a very convenient tool for this purpose.

In the drawings from figures 1 to 8 inclusive, I show the steps to lay out and make a through-dovetail joint in chronological order. These operations entail the use of a band saw to remove the waste in both tail and pin members of the joint. Figure 4 shows how to remove the waste from the tail member. If this waste is carefully sawed out without crossing over the guidelines, very little trimming with a chisel or file is needed to true up the saw cuts.

When the saw cuts on the tail member are smooth enough to use as a pattern for laying out the angles on the pin member, place the tail member over the end of the pin member and mark these angels as in figure 5. Some cabinet-makers prefer to make and cut out the pin member of a dovetail joint and then lay out the tail member from it, but I greatly prefer doing it as I show it here. To me this method is much easier. After marking the angles using the method shown in figure 5, true up the lines with the protractor, and then draw the remaining guidelines with a try square to remove the waste from the pin member. Although I've seen instructions for laying out guidelines [X] in figure 5, which are drawn across the grain with a marking gauge, I never use a marking gauge to draw these lines. Gauge lines here are difficult, if not impossible, to remove after the joint is made, while pencil lines can be erased or sanded to remove.

Most of the waste to be removed from the pin member can be cut out with a band saw. Study the procedure used in figure 7. Before removing the waste, however, use a dovetail saw (see fig. 6) to start all angle cuts. Be sure when sawing these angles to saw down on the waste side of the line, so the pins will not be reduced in size. Do step 6 before step 7, and the remaining small wedges can then be removed with a coping saw as done in figure 8. If you do not have access to a band saw, you can remove all of the leftover waste with a coping saw, after the angle cuts have been made with the dovetail saw.

A half-lap multiple dovetail joint, like the one in figure 9, requires a little more time and care than a through-dovetail joint. In this type of joint, the waste must be chiseled out on the pin section, as shown in figure 11. I use a ½-inch-chisel with a bevel-edged blade to do most of this trimming, and on work where these mortises are smaller, I do most of this trimming with a ¼-inch-woodcarving chisel with its thin blade. The beveled blade is better than a square-edged socket-firmer chisel to do dovetail work, because its thin edges make it easier to trim the sharp angles. In figure 11 I have put numbers on the chisels to indicate the sequence to be followed when trimming out the waste.

Drawer fronts with protruding lips, like those shown in figure 12, require still greater care. With patience and time, you should have no difficulty making these joints. Be very careful when making these joints to figure measurements and drawer clearance very accurately so the drawer will slide easily into its opening when put together. The chances to plane drawer sides to get a better fit are practically nil after the drawer joints have been glued together. Notice too that no lip is made to protrude on the lower edge of the drawer front on such drawers, even though all four edges have molding on the drawer face.

ABOUT THE AUTHOR

Franklin H. Gottshall is a contributing editor to **The American Woodworker.**

Excerpted with permission from **Masterpiece Furniture Making** *- Stackpole Books, Harrisburg, PA. Copyright 1979 by Franklin Gottshall.*

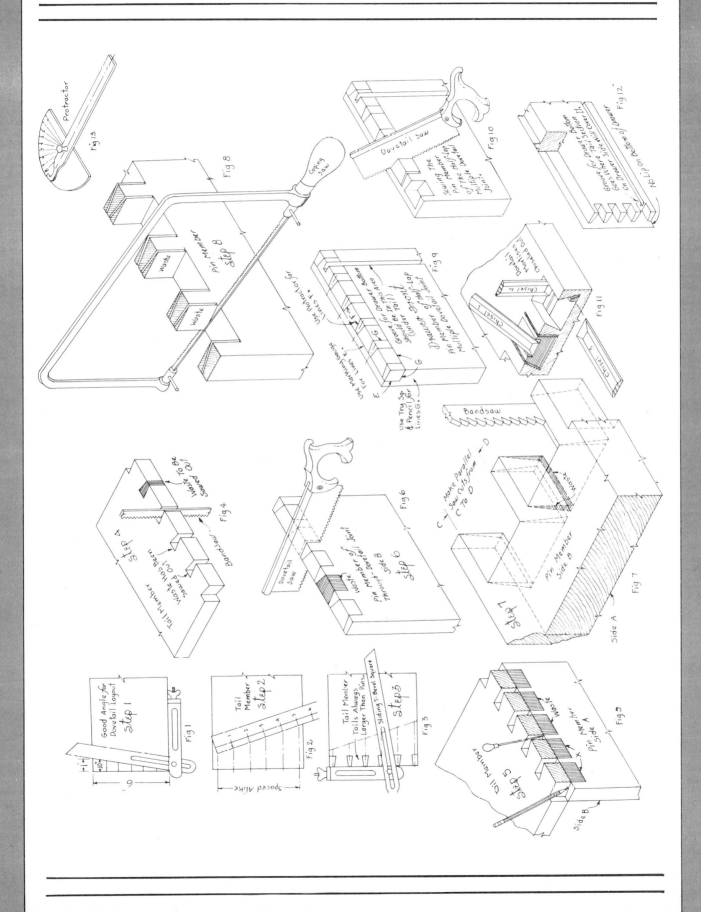

Fig 13 — Protractor

Fig 8 — Step 8, Pin Member, Waste, Waste, Use Protractor for Lines

Coping Saw

Fig 10 — Dovetail Saw, Sawing the Pin Member Half Lap of the Multiple Dovetail Joint

Fig 12 — Groove for Drawer Bottom Goes Where Side will cover It. No LIP on Bottom of Drawer

Fig 9 — Groove for Drawer Bottom, Groove for Pin Tail should Be Tail, Drawer Front Half-Lap Pin Member Dovetail Joint Multiple Dovetail Joint. Use Try Sq. & Pencil for Lines G. Use Marking Gauge for Lines E.

Fig 11 — Dovetail Mortises Chiseled Out, Chisel, Chisel

Fig 4 — Step A, Waste To Be Sawed Out, Tail Member, Waste Has Been Spaced Out, Bandsaw, Ho Pamos

Fig 6 — Step 6, Dovetail Saw, Waste of Joint, Pin Member of Joint Through Dovetail Side B

Bandsaw — Fig 7, Step 7, Make Parallel Saw Cuts from C To D, Pin Member Side B, Side A, Waste

Fig 1 — Step 1, Good Angle for Dovetail Layout, 10°, 6

Fig 2 — Step 2, Tail Member, Spaced Alike, 1 2 3 4 5

Fig 3 — Step 3, Tail Member, Tails Always Larger Than Pins, Sliding T-Bevel Square

Fig 5 — Step 5, Pin Member Side A, Waste, Tail Member, Side B

Dovetails

There May Still Be Something To Learn

One of the most publicized of all woodworking joints, the dovetail has certainly created a love affair with many woodworkers. It has also struck fear in the hearts of those "lions" of the craft. A number of different methods can be used to lay out and make the joint. In this article, two different authors discuss some of their ideas concerning the dovetail.

Tips For Successful Handcut Dovetails

by W. Curtis Johnson

Accurate sawing is the key to successful handcut dovetails. Begin by sawing little squares to gain the control necessary to split a line while keeping the saw perpendicular to the board. Pictured are some of the squares cut by the author as he gained the ability to produce dovetails.

If you are like me, you probably read half a dozen articles on handcut dovetails before attempting to saw them for the first time. And, if you are like me, all that reading didn't make your initial sets of dovetails fit. The purpose of this article is to provide extra details that will make it easier for you to be successful. The extra steps will slow down your production rate, but a beginner just wants the joint to fit and can afford a little extra time. Although through dovetails are discussed here, the methods are easily generalized to half-blind and full-blind dovetails. I will assume that you have already read an article on the basics of dovetail joints such as "How To Lay Out and Make Dovetail Joints" by Franklin H. Gottshall.

Dovetail joints demand accurate sawing. This is one joint that is not cut oversize and then trimmed. The idea is to saw correctly the first time so the joint fits snugly. Prepare for accurate sawing by furnishing good lighting. I bought one of those inexpensive action-arm desk lamps and installed it in a hole drilled in my workbench. I can move it around to put the lighting just where I need it. A magnifier also makes a tremendous difference, but don't go overboard. A magnification of 1.5x is plenty since you will focus closer to the work. If you don't normally wear glasses, try low power reading glasses from your local drug store. Woodworkers who already wear

Mark both faces and the edge of a board to cut ³/₄ inch squares ¹/₄ of an inch thick. Use a scratch awl rather than a pencil (used here for clarity in the photo). Check each practice cut for accuracy and squareness. When you have mastered sawing, you are ready to handcut a set of dovetails.

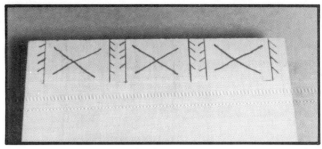

Here the pins are marked out showing the system for ensuring against cutting on the wrong side of a line. The idea is not to cut any pencil mark. A scratch awl should be used to mark the vertical lines as a pencil (used here for clarity) is usually too wide for the required accuracy.

corrective lenses prefer flip-up units that are worn on the head (these can be ordered from Edroy Products, 130 West 29th St., New York, NY 10001).

Now that you can actually see what you are sawing, it is time to practice. Don't start with dovetails because too much time is spent on relatively simple tasks like marking them out and cleaning out the waste. Instead, choose a square, surfaced board and mark a depth line on both faces about ³/₄ of an inch from one end. Don't worry about the dovetail angle yet. Use a square to mark for saw cuts that are perpendicular to both the end and face of the board. Mark both the face and the end with a sharp scratch awl for a series of cuts about ¹/₄ of an inch apart.

Place your fine toothed dovetail saw on one side of the line so that the edge of the teeth will split the line down the middle. Put your thumb against the end of the board and against the saw just above the teeth to steady and guide it. Draw the saw gently backwards to start the cut. Saw carefully and remove the little square you have created. Now, check the cut for accuracy and squareness in both directions. Try again, concentrating on any problems. Try sawing on both sides of the line. I practiced for half an hour every night and produced a lot of little squares before I could routinely saw with the required accuracy. Once you have mastered this skill, it will not take long to master sawing for the pins at an 80 degree angle across the end and sawing for the tails at an 80 degree angle along the face. Practice the angled cuts in a similar way.

As you begin practicing you will probably find that your saw skips as you try to start it and that it chatters in the kerf. It is a poor workman indeed who blames his tools. Nevertheless, these difficulties are probably the fault of the

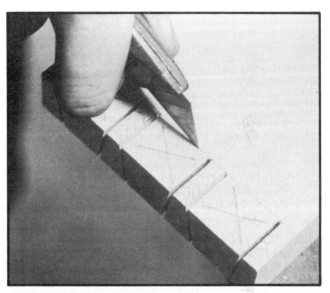

Deepen the depth line at the waste with a sharp knife, but make it a moderate cut so that you don't widen the line. Start at the edge of the waste and score only to the center to avoid accidentally cutting into a tail or pin.

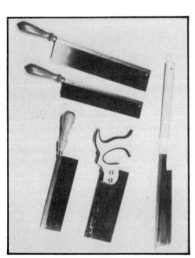

Various types of dovetail saws are available. Pictured here from top to bottom, left to right: standard Continental saw, Continental saw with thin blade, short Continental (Gent's) saw, English saw, and Japanese pull-cut saw.

saw. Sad to say, there are few tools, either hand or power, that will perform properly as purchased. A good workman takes the time to tune each of his tools. Your saw was probably sharpened to crosscut even though dovetailing is a ripping operation, and the teeth, undoubtedly, have too much set for smooth sawing. Also, the blade may well be warped and require straightening. Clamp the saw blade in a vice between two pieces of steel to reduce the set. Then have the saw sharpened for ripping. It will still crosscut nicely in hardwood. Try to find someone who will hand file your saw. This will cost more than machine sharpening, but the saw will work better. Be sure to warn the person doing the sharpening that you want only the absolute minimum set. The kerf should be just wide enough to allow correction should you get started at the wrong angle.

The type of dovetail saw to use is really a matter of personal taste. Japanese dovetail saws come sharp and with the proper set. They cut smoothly, but their long teeth are weak. They are not easily resharpened, and the sawdust they make obscures the cutting lines since they cut on the pull stroke. The small dovetail saws preferred by Continental woodworkers can be tuned to cut well. However, the saws with

Remove a chip at the depth line after scoring to retain a crisp edge. Follow this procedure twice. Both the initial scoring and the deep scoring are shown here.

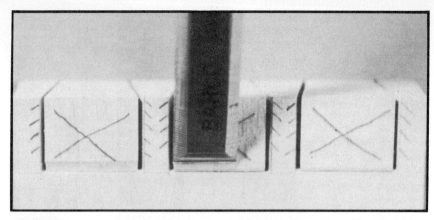

exceptionally thin blades can only be used on thin boards because the blades tend to bend with the grain of the wood. I prefer an English dovetail saw with its full handle. These are fairly expensive, and the one I received from a mail order company was warped, so I had to bend it straight. It also had crosscut teeth and too much set to saw smoothly.

The method used to mark the boards can improve your chance of success. Use a marking gauge to score the depth line so that you have a registration mark to accurately form the edges that will seat against the face of the other board. If you wish to incorporate this line into the design produced by the dovetails, it should be scored deeply, and the depth line should be about 1/64th of an inch further from the end than the thickness of the mating board. With this system the protruding ends need only be sanded flush to finish the joint. To remove the line, just break the surface of the face, and the depth line should be the same distance from the end as the thickness of the mating board. The marks will have to be planed from the faces, but the planing will push the end grain against the other surfaces and remove rounded edges to give a crisp look.

The all-metal No. 90 marking gauge by Stanley is much easier to use than the wooden ones, but regardless of the model, this is another tool that needs to be tuned. The round point on the pin is made for marking along the grain and must be modified to cut the wood fibers when marking across the grain. File the point straight across the front and diagonally across the back (next to the depth adjustment) to form a sharp edge that will cut as you draw the gauge toward you. The diagonal across the back will force the edge of the board against the depth adjustment. As an alternative, some woodworkers may prefer to use a square and knife to score the depth line.

Having sawed more than once on the wrong side of a line, I now do more than simply mark the waste with an ''X''. I make short dashes that just touch the cutting line. The idea is not to cut any mark.

The crisp, straight edge formed by scoring the depth line and removing a chip will fit snugly against the mating board. It also provides a base for removing the waste and cleaning up with a slight undercut.

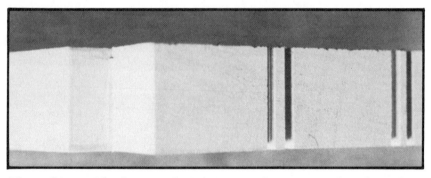

Three chips guide the saw when removing the waste at the edges of the board with the tails. Use a chisel to clean up the end grain inside the clean edges and undercut slightly for a perfect fit.

Here is the setup for making the tails from the pins.

It is not easy to remove the waste and still retain a crisp edge across the grain. Use the registration provided by the depth line to guide a sharp knife in scoring at the waste. Begin at the saw kerf and score only halfway across to avoid accidentally cutting the corner of a pin or tail. The knife should cut only to a moderate depth that does not widen the line. Remove a chip from the waste to form a "V". Repeat this to deepen a crisp, straight edge that will fit snugly against the mating board. The waste itself can be removed in any manner that is convenient. When this method is applied to all three sides of the waste at the edges of the board with the tails, the V's guide the saw when removing the waste. Clean up the end grain inside the clean edge that was formed by scoring, undercutting slightly.

Pins or tails, which should be cut first? The experts are evenly divided on this. Since I'm more likely to make a mistake at this point, my preference is to cut the pins first. Most errors will be hidden because the tails will be marked from the pins. I also find it easier to mark the tails from the pins than vice versa. Clamp one edge of a nicely planed and squared 2 x 4 along the depth line on the board to receive the tails. Then clamp the board with the completed pins into position for marking. Use a metal scratch awl or a hard and very sharp pencil to get a fine, accurate line.

Test the joint after you have cut the pins and tails, removed the waste, and cleaned up the seats. First, bevel the inside edges of the tails to ease the entry of the pins. Obviously, the bevel cannot extend to the end or it will show. Put a clamp on the board with the pins on the far side of the depth line to prevent possible splitting, although the joint really shouldn't be that tight. Carefully tap the joint together. If any contact is too tight, pare it with a chisel and try again. When the joint goes completely together, the trick is to separate it again without destroying the fit. Clamp the board with the tails in a vice with the other board resting on the bench top. Use a small board shaped like the pins as a driver and gently tap the joint apart a bit at a time.

Glue swells wood, so you cannot paint the joint with glue and expect it to go together. Put a small line of glue just inside the back of the tails (on the bevels) and just inside the ends of the pins. As the joint is assembled, plenty of glue will be spread into the joint.

One of the nice properties of wood is that it is relatively easy to repair errors. I'm not referring to sawdust and glue, which invariably looks terrible. Instead, save all the scraps from your project. When a fit is poor or there is a big dent, hunt up a scrap with perfectly matching grain, cut a small piece of wood to fit, and glue it into place. If one of the contacts is loose when testing, glue a scrap to the tail and try again. Choose carefully and match the end grain. If there is a small gap after the joint is glued, slice a wedge shaped shav-

Test the fit of your dovetail joint. A clamp on the board with the pins helps prevent splitting, but the joint should go together easily with only a few taps.

Use a driver to gently tap the dovetail joint apart without destroying the fit.

ing with a knife and fit it into the gap with a little glue. Done in this way, almost any repair will be invisible — even to you.

If you've read a number of articles on dovetails, you know that each author has his own methods. With so many ways to make a successful joint, the inescapable conclusion is that it can't be too difficult. The keys are to tune your tools, practice sawing until it is second nature, and develop some techniques to avoid common errors.

ABOUT THE AUTHOR:
W. Curtis Johnson is a woodworker living in Corvallis, Oregon. He is a frequent contributor to **The American Woodworker.**

Dovetails

Some Time Saving Tips

by Mac Campbell

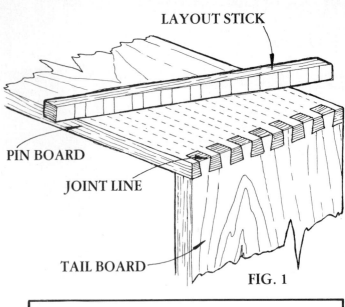

LAYOUT STICK

PIN BOARD

JOINT LINE

TAIL BOARD

FIG. 1

Laying Out Dovetails

Hand-cut dovetails have much to recommend themselves to the custom or limited production woodworker. They are (when properly laid out and cut) an extremely strong joint, and they can add a pleasing and distinctive appearance to a piece. This sets the piece apart from large-scale production pieces, and as such, is often a useful selling point. Unfortunately, dovetails are not without drawbacks. They are tedious to lay out and cut, and the scribe lines used in the traditional layout method can be difficult to remove. The system described below has been worked out to ease some of these drawbacks while retaining the positive aspects of the joint.

The heart of the system lies in establishing a standard ratio between pins and tails at the joint line (see Figure 1). This is largely a matter of personal taste. A ratio of about 2 to 5 is a good choice. On a straight stick of wood that is longer than the width of any panels likely to be joined (the "layout stick"), put a series of marks in this proportion (i.e., one mark at the end, then another 2 cm away, then another 5 cm further on, then 2 cm, etc.). Other proportions can be marked on other sides of the stick.

To lay out the joint itself, place the layout stick across the outside of the pin board in such a way that the edge of the board lines up with the outside of a pin (see Figure 1). Note that the angle at which the stick is laid across the board determines the size of the dovetails, even though their proportion remains unchanged. Transfer the marks from the stick to the board, and then, using either a square or a marking gauge, carry them down to the joint line. More elaborate patterns of dovetails can be obtained simply by using one angle of the stick for the outside quarter of the board, then a different angle for the center portion. The variations are endless and easily obtained.

"...Dovetails...can add a pleasing and distinctive appearance to a piece..."

It is not necessary to mark out all cuts of the dovetail, but it is a good idea to indicate clearly which sections are waste. Set a cutting gauge from the tail board (thickness of the tail board plus about 1/64"), but scribe only the *inside* of the pin board. Scribe this line quite deeply. To aid in setting

up the table saw, scribe a piece of scrap wood at the same setting. Place the dado head on the table saw so that it is more than ½ the width of the wide end of the tails, but not quite as wide as the narrow end. (If you have laid out dovetails of varying widths, this may not be possible. In this case set the dado head to just under the width of the narrow end of the *narrowest* tail. You will probably have to make multiple passes to clean out the wider tail slots.) Set the height of the dado head so that it cuts to the center of the scribed line. This is where the scribed piece of scrap comes in handy. An auxiliary fence on the miter gauge and a second miter gauge in the other slot in the saw table, help considerably in keeping everything square and steady. Set the miter gauge(s) to the preferred angle for the dovetails. A 1 to 6 ratio, or about 10°, is traditional. Run the pin board through the table saw on end, cutting one side of each pin. After all pieces have had one side of the pins cut, set the miter gauge to 10° the other way and cut the other side.

Once the pins have been cut, tails are marked and cut in the usual manner. Preferably, make the side cuts on the band saw, remove most of the waste with a coping saw, then clean up with mallet and chisel.

After a bit of practice, use of this system will cut in half the time required to produce a through dovetail joint. The time reduction will be even greater when a project involves cutting multiples of the joint in several pieces. Systems which allow this type of time reduction are rare enough in the woodworking shop; systems which also produce a noticeable increase in accuracy, as this one will, are rare indeed.

ABOUT THE AUTHOR:
Mac Campbell is a professional woodworker living in New Brunswick. He owns and operates a custom woodworking shop.

Making Through Dovetails With A Band Saw

by W. Curtis Johnson

The jig for sawing pins also moves with the work. The jig is not needed if your table tilts in both directions.

The endgrain of through dovetails provides a decorative element which speaks of craftsmanship. The intriguing pattern created by the alternating pins and tails is as pleasing as it is strong. The band saw, and its cousin the jig saw, provide an alternative method for cutting through dovetails while retaining the flexibility normally associated with hand work. The method described here is particularly simple, accurate, and well suited to both beginners and experts.

The method described below has all the versatility of hand sawing.

The band saw and jig saw are gentle tools which are the mechanized version of the hand saw. They are easy to use because the table provides precision alignment while the addition of a miter gauge and fence provide repeatability. If the table on your motor-driven saw tilts to the left as well as to the right, only one simple jig is needed for mechanical alignment of the cuts. If your table tilts only to the right, a second jig will be necessary to provide both directions of tilt. The method described below has all the versatility of hand sawing and a number of advantages beyond ease of alignment and repeat-

ability. A bevel gauge is not needed, only the outside face of the board will have to be marked for pins and tails, it will not be necessary to mark the end grain, and a sharp pencil will supply easy-to-see marks with the required accuracy.

A variable taper-cutting device is used to make the jigs for cutting dovetails. Choose a piece of stable and straight grained wood to make the angled parts of the jigs. Dress the board on both sides and both edges. Set the taper-cutting device to the angle that you use for dovetails (I prefer 80 degrees, a 1 to 6 ratio). The jig for sawing the tails is 15 inches long and is ripped from the board so that it tapers from one inch to 3½ inches. The tapered edge will contact the work and must move with it. Attach a strip of 150 grit sandpaper to prevent slipping. The two faces and the other edge of the jig must slide, so wax them well. If your mechanical saw tilts to both sides, this is the only jig you will need.

A second jig will provide the tilt for cutting the pins when the table is in the horizontal position. It will give both right and left tilts, depending on its orientation. Since the table remains in its normal position, some workers may prefer to use this jig even though their saw table tilts to both sides. While you are at it, you should probably make a few versions of this jig for work of various widths. A 6-inch jig will handle work up to 9 inches wide. A 12-inch jig will handle work up to 16 inches wide. Two tapered boards form the sides of each jig. Rip them from the original piece of straight grained wood by using the fence alternately with and without the taper jig. These tapered boards should be about ¼ inch at the narrow end. Cut them to length so that the members of each pair have identical heights. The base of the jig is ¼ inch plywood. One dimension should be the length of the tapered board (6 inches and 12 inches for the two jigs discussed above). The other dimension should be one inch less than your table extends in front of the blade (5 and ½ inches for my saw). Glue the tapered boards along the two corresponding sides of one face. Be sure the tapers face in the same direction. The tapered edges will contact the work and move with it. Again, glue strips of 150 grit sandpaper to these edges to prevent slipping. Attach a smoothly finished ¾ × 1½ inch board to span corresponding ends of the tapered boards. Countersunk flat head screws will secure these pieces which will ride against the fence. The piece at the narrow ends of the tapers also serves to register and secure the work. Wax the bottom of the base and the two boards which will contact the fence so they slide smoothly. Your jigs for cutting dovetails are now complete.

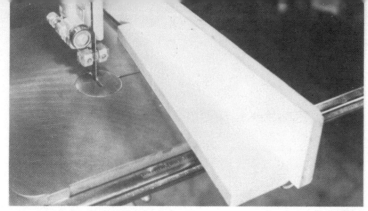

The jig for sawing the tails on a band saw cocks the work at an angle. It moves with the work, sliding against the fence.

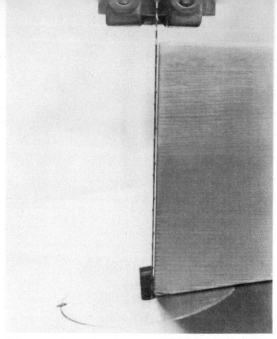

It is easy to determine the proper tilt of the table with the jig for cutting the tails. The teeth on the blade appear to climb up the full length of the end.

Now you are ready to make any set of through dovetail joints. Dress the boards to be dovetailed in the normal way so they are flat and square. Special attention should be paid to the end grain which will serve as the registration and the inside face which should receive its final surfacing. Mark the boards to differentiate the inside from the outside.

Use a marking gauge suitable for scoring across the grain to cut the depth lines. When scoring for the pins, the gauge should be set for the thickness of the board which will have the tails and vice versa. The exact setting is a matter of personal preference. If you plan to retain this line in the final product, it is probably best to set the gauge to have the end grain protrude slightly above the face. Later, it will be easy to sand the end grain flush with the face. If you plan to remove the depth line, then plan on flush end grain to facilitate planing. Cut depth lines completely around the board which will have the tails. It is only necessary to cut depth lines on the faces of the board which will have the pins.

Plan the layout of your joint. There is infinite flexibility with this method so you can afford to be creative. Tails are usually cut wider than pins, but the exact ratio and the number of elements can be tailored to the effect you wish to achieve. Moreover, the sizes can vary across the joint. Remember to end the joint at both sides with pins. (Here I am not varying the dimensions.) My pins are ¼ inch on their narrow face and my tails are one inch at the end grain.

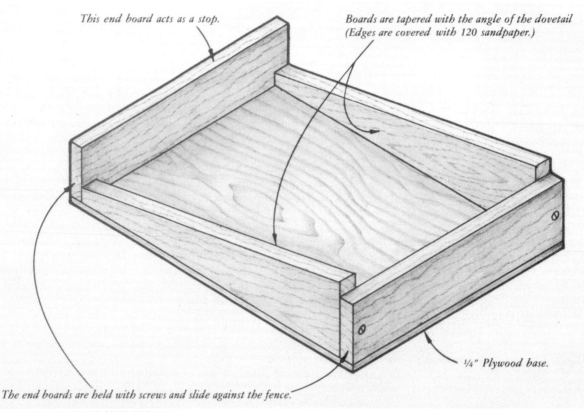

This end board acts as a stop.

Boards are tapered with the angle of the dovetail (Edges are covered with 120 sandpaper.)

¼" Plywood base.

The end boards are held with screws and slide against the fence.

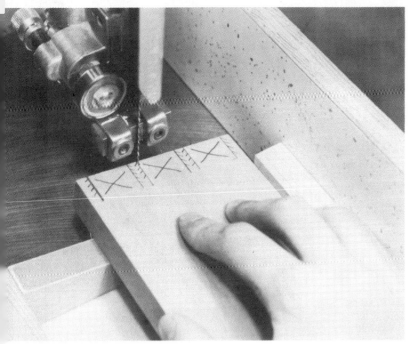

Use of the jig for sawing pins is illustrated for the first set of cuts.

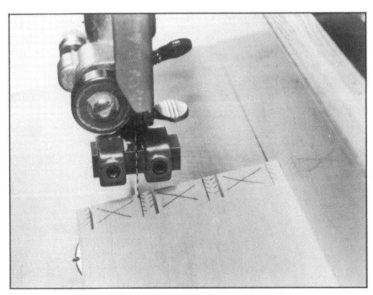

Cutting the pins with the table tilted is illustrated here for the second set of cuts. You will want to choose between tilting the table or using the jig and not combine the two options as I did here for illustrative purposes.

Mark the position of the pins since they will be cut first. My work is usually planned and dimensioned in advance, so I use a sliding square for this purpose. A sharp pencil will provide sufficient accuracy. You need only mark one face, and I choose the narrow side of the pins. Even after marking the waste I find it all too easy to cut on the wrong side of the line, especially when there are many joints to be done. Thus, in addition to marking the waste with an X, I add some angled marks on the face of the pin which just touch each line. The idea here is to saw on the waste side of the line and never saw a pencil line. The angled lines also indicate the shape of the pin to avoid confusion on this critical point.

If you are not using the jig for the pins, you will have to tilt the table of your saw to the proper angle. This is easily accomplished by placing the tapered edge of the jig for cutting the tails on the table. Put the large end of the device close to and just in front of the saw blade. Sight along the end of the jig and tilt the table until the teeth on the blade appear to climb up the full length of the end. The tilt on your table will be identical to the angle of the jig. Use your fence to line up the proper side of each pin with the saw blade. If you don't have a fence, clamp a straight board to your table. Be sure the shape of the pin coincides with the tilt of the blade. Extreme accuracy is not necessary at this point since the tails will be marked from the pins. Saw corresponding pins for all the joints before moving the fence for the next cut. After cutting one side of each pin, reverse the tilt and cut the other side of each pin in the same manner.

The waste can be removed by chopping with a chisel in the normal way. However, the relatively wide kerf of the mechanized saw blade can be used to advantage here. I deepen the depth line slightly at the waste with a sharp narrow knife and remove a small chip with a chisel. Then I repeat the process, scoring deeply. This gives me a good clean edge which is perpendicular to the face and is not moved inward by the bevel of a chisel. With the wider kerf, it is easy to insert a coping saw and remove the waste. The smooth accurate base created by the knife provides a foundation for paring out the remainder of the waste and cleaning up the corners.

The tails are marked from the pins. The boards are held in place with clamps and a squared 2 × 4, and a sharp pencil puts a line into the corner.

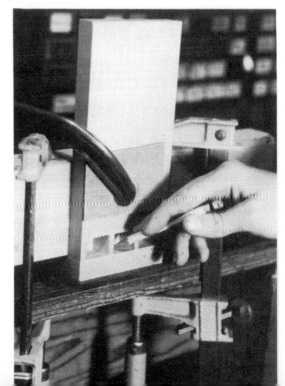

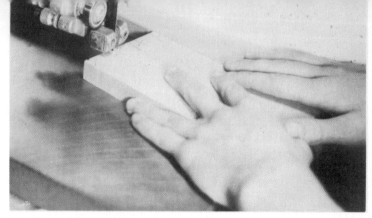

The jig provides accurate sawing of the tails. Saw into the waste moving the jig with the work to maintain the proper angle. Moving the work forward relative to the jig puts the blade closer to the line.

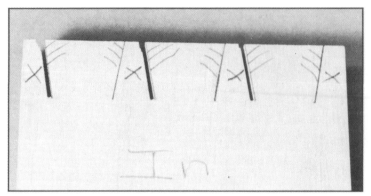

Here is the first set of cuts for the tails. This illustrates the marking and the cuts which progressively move toward the edge of the line.

The finished dovetail joint.

The tails are now marked from the pins with which they will mate. Mark each joint so that there will be no confusion about the proper pairs later on. I use a carefully squared 2 × 4 to position the two pieces in each pair. The 2 inch face is placed on the inside face of the board to receive the tails, just inside the depth line. The two are clamped to the workbench with the edge of the 2 × 4 splitting the depth line. The other board forming this joint is clamped to the 4 inch face with the mating pins firmly against the board to be marked for the tails. Be sure that the wide face of the pins is toward the inside of the joint and that the mark extends completely into the corner since you will be cutting along this edge of the line. If necessary, sharpen the pencil with some sandpaper. Mark all the tails for all the joints and mark the waste in the same way that you did for the pins.

Now the precision alignment provided by the saw table combines with the precision alignment possible with the fence and the jig to produce tails which will accurately match the corresponding pins. Place the jig for the tails next to your saw fence and adjust the fence so that the blade cuts into the waste next to the first tail. Needless to say, the jig must be oriented so its taper is the same as the angle to be cut. Make trial cuts into the waste, moving the jig with the work and creep up on the mark with each trial by sliding the work forward relative to the jig. The jig is positioned correctly when the kerf just skims the pencil line. This is easy to judge if your saw table is well lighted. Cut the tail but stop just before the depth line. Here the wide kerf is a disadvantage. If you cut to the depth line you will have trouble cleaning up the corners. After you have cut one angle for all the tails, reverse the jig and cut the other angle.

Remove the waste in between the tails as you did for the pins. Since you stopped each cut before reaching the depth line, this registration mark will guide your knife right to the corner of the tail as you score the depth line. The base left by the knife will make cleaning the corners easy in spite of the wide kerf. Similarly, knife around the depth line at the waste for each end before sawing it off. These saw cuts can be smoothed with a chisel to the accurate base created by the knife for a perfect fit. Your through dovetails are complete.

Tap together mating pairs of pins and tails to check the fit of each joint. If any part is too tight, trim the tail on the saw using the jig to creep up on the mark. The lines on the assembled joint should be tight and have a crisp look. Take the joint apart by tapping on a thin board fit to the shape of a pin. Put glue only on the ends of the pins for final assembly. Clamp the tails gently but firmly to bring the tails snugly against the base between the pins.

ABOUT THE AUTHOR: *W. Curtis Johnson is a contributing editor to* **The American Woodworker.**

The Fairing Batten

by Tom Liebl

As a boat moves through the water, any humps or hollows in its hull cause turbulence and drag, slowing her down. Boatbuilders will take great pains to ensure that a boat's hull, with all its complex curves, will be "sweet and fair".

The same techniques used to produce a fair hull will give the furniture maker curves that the hand and eye travel over as smoothly as a boat over water.

In the shop, it's very tempting to reach for a soup or coffee can or grab a router with a round-over bit to quickly radius a corner or an edge. If we take a moment to reconsider, a curve of changing radius (elipse, hyperbola, etc.) may make a more effective design statement.

To my eye, a circle or its arc represents a focal point. I avoid them if I want my eye to flow over a piece. Beyond that, curves can become very subjective. Usually, I am faced with two or three fixed points that can be connected by whatever curve suits me. The variables are countless, and I necessrily become very involved in the design process. Chairwork, in particular, demands complex curves to reflect the complex curves of the human body. No curve will be fully effective, however, unless it is smooth and uninterrupted. To that end, we can make good use of the boatbuilders' friend, the fairing batten.

A fairing batten is simply a length of material that, when sprung into a curve, will produce a line free of defect. Wood, plastic, and metal will all work well as batten stock depending upon the severity of the curve. For the boatbuilder, clear straight-grained white pine is the wood of choice with oak and mahogany being used on tighter curves. Draftsmen often use plastic battens called splines. Splines are useful in the shop as well as on the drawing board. Bandsaw blades are handy for very tight work.

Wood makes the most versatile batten. It can be slash-scarfed to any length, and its section, and therefore flexibility, can be modified quickly. Care should be taken when making a batten; try to keep it straight and true as any kinks can disrupt a line. Sometimes a batten is painted flat black to increase contrast, but normally they are left unfinished.

If a batten is used and stored with care it will last indefinitely. Avoid nailing through the batten whenever possible. Do not bend the batten beyond its ability to spring back. Store the batten well supported on a rack with even air circulation.

Whatever the material, the batten should be as stiff as practical for the situation at hand; this will give a fairer line between control points. On flat surfaces, battens are usually

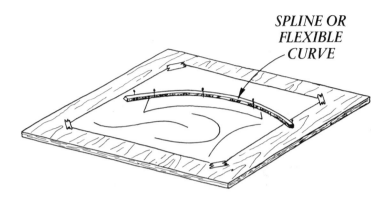

SPLINE OR FLEXIBLE CURVE

bent around nails or pins driven along their edges. Boat designers use lead weights called "ducks" to avoid the holes made by pins. Battens are typically rectangular in section and bent on the flat, although on curved surfaces, they are nearer to square in section and are nailed through.

A good rule is the fewer the nails the fairer the curve. Let the batten and your eye find the right line. It is important to allow the batten to extend well beyond the endpoints of whatever is being drawn while continuing the curve, either increasing or decreasing in radius. This will help prevent dreaded "flat spots" near the ends and will give a much more fluid line.

It is well to spend some time fiddling with a curve. Although the batten is a great aid, finding a fair curve is a skill that takes time to develop. View the batten from all angles. One trick is to bend over and look at the curve from between your legs; this disorienting process allows more complete concentration on the line. In that same vein, while drawing a familiar object such as a chair, view it upside down to minimize any preconceived notions of its shape. Appraisal and reappraisal are needed because seemingly insignificant adjustments of the batten can produce a curve that will suddenly be "just right".

With practice comes speed and confidence. With the aid of the fairing batten, we can move beyond the limits of geometric construction as easily as drawing a circle with a compass.

ABOUT THE AUTHOR:
Tom Liebl is an experienced boat builder and cabinetmaker from Wisconsin.

The Basics of Steam Bending

by Chris Becksvoort

There is something fascinating about bent wood. A material that ordinarily grows in a more or less straight line is transformed into graceful arches or flowing curves. Getting wood into a curve can be achieved in several ways: sawing, stacking, kerfing or laminating. Yet the most popular, as well as the oldest, is a combination of heat and moisture — steam. The process of steam bending has been used by boat builders in all parts of the world for thousands of years.

Most woodworkers, after conquering the basics of tool use, joinery, and construction, eventually look for greater challenges to broaden their horizons. Many eventually dabble in steam bending, with varying degrees of success. Like other facets of working with wood, successful steam bending depends on theory, knowledge of the material, practice, and the experience gained from past failures.

Theory

In theory, wood bending is quite simple. The wood is plasticized, through the use of steam, so that the cells become

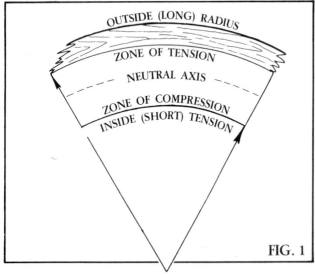

FIG. 1

flexible enough to allow the wood to bend. The bend is held by means of a jig until the wood dries and the individual cells retain their new shape.

In a simple bend (Figure 1) the inside radius of the curve is under compression, the approximate center is neutral, and the outside radius is under tension. Thus, the wood must stretch, since the outside radius is longer than the inside radius, where the cells are forced together into a shorter curve. The process of steaming allows compression of the wood cells 25% to 30% *beyond* the normal limits.

Wood Selection

The biggest single factor determining the success of a bend is the selection of the stock: the species, the grain, the the moisture content. The first consideration should be which species to use. Some woods bend relatively well, others not at all. Generally, the hardwoods bend better than softwoods. There is no single "best" bending wood. Two criteria are used to determine bendability. First, wood is judged on the percentage of unbroken pieces. For instance, if a run of 100 one inch white oak pieces produces 91 perfect bends, and a run of 100 one inch pieces of rock maple produces 57 perfect bends, the 91% success rate of white oak is better than the 57% of maple (Table A). On the other hand, a percentage tells little of a wood's ability to bend into tight curves. Consequently, another method is also used to describe bendability: the limiting radii of curvature (the tightest bend possible without failure) both supported with straps and unsupported. The woods most often used in commercial bending operations are red oak, white oak, elm, hickory, ash, beech, birch, and walnut. Of the softwoods, yew, cedars (both Alaskan and Atlantic white), Douglas fir, southern yellow pine, and redwood are sometimes used in boat work, but only for moderate bends.

Once the desired species has been chosen, the second most important consideration is the grain — more specifically, the orientation of the grain, in regards to the length of the piece being bent. First and foremost, the grain should be as straight as possible. The old Windsor chairmakers would "rive" (split) their stock, not saw it, to ensure that the grain would run straight throughout the entire piece. Grain run-out (grain running diagonally from one edge to the other) of greater than 1 inch in 15 should not be used. The closer the grain comes to running the full length of the bend, the greater the chances of success. Regarding the actual orientation of grain in the bend, I have had better luck with flat sawn stock. That is, the growth rings should be parallel to the bending jig (Figure 2).

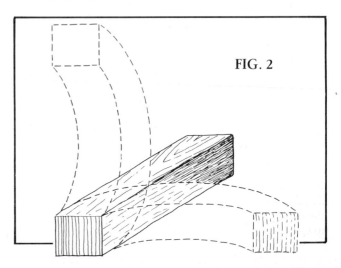

FIG. 2

After the stock has been selected for straight grain, any pieces with knots, rot, checks, or brashness should be discarded. It is also a good idea to run a slight chamfer of 1/16'' to 1/8'' on all four corners to prevent splits from starting. A pass or two with a block plane will suffice. Stock should be surfaced on four sides to ensure uniform thickness. Any additional time spent in scrutinizing, selecting, and preparing the stock is well worthwhile.

The last consideration in stock selection is moisture content. It is well known that green wood bends better than dried wood. Try breaking a small branch off a tree. Depending on species and thickness, it can be bent back on itself with no trouble. Yet even green wood is not ideal for bending. The moisture in the cell walls makes them more pliable, but the water inside the cells keeps them from bending as much as possible. Research has shown that wood between 15-20% moisture content is ideal for bending. The fiber saturation point (when water has dried out of cell cavities, but not the cell walls) is around 30%. So, at 15-20%, some of the water has dried out of the cell walls, yet they are still pliable. I have had good luck with moisture contents as high as 25%. It should be remembered that below the fiber saturation, the wood starts to shrink, and that using wood with 20% moisture content will result in considerably more shrinkage than wood at 15% moisture content. Most wood available to woodworkers today is kiln dried to 6% moisture content and will usually be 8-10% by the time it is delivered. To bring the moisture content up to 15-20%, the wood can be left outside during humid weather, or can be soaked in water for a few hours prior to steaming.

"...Water can be boiled by whatever method is cheapest or most convenient..."

Equipment

A steam source, a box, and jigs are necessary to begin the operation. The size and expense of these depend on the size of the stock to be bent, and the number of times the operation will be performed. A one time setup for six custom chairs would be entirely different from a production chair or boat run. I have done one time antique repairs with only a tea kettle, no steam box, and a form cut out of a 12'' pine board.

Water can be boiled by whatever method is cheapest or most convenient. Electricity is probably the easiest for small jobs. A tea kettle or pressure cooker on a hot plate, or a wallpaper steamer are the old standbys. If you have a wood stove, a five gallon can with a safety valve and hose nozzle will do. Some larger commercial operations use LP gas. A camping stove or even a kerosene heater will also work. One boat yard I visited had a boiler made from a beer keg; another used a gas hot water heater.

The shape of the steam box depends on the size of the stock to be bent. A box 1 x 1 x 4 feet serves well for most chair work. Three-quarter-inch AC exterior plywood makes a good material. Corners can be screwed. Doors with gaskets can be attached at both ends if desired. A hose nipple is inserted near the middle and a drain nipple at the bottom, or low end. The hose from the boiler to the steam box should be as short and straight as possible. Avoid long lengths, kinks and loops, as this invites condensation in the hose. A rack inside the tank is needed to keep the members being steamed apart, to ensure good steam distribution. Metal should be avoided.

One of my first steam boxes was stove pipe, which turned the oak slats a dark gray-blue color. Instead of doors, boat builders stuff rags into both ends of the steam box. This allows very long stock to be steamed in a short box, if only a small section is actually being bent. For instance, if an 8 foot piece is being bent into a right angle, only the 2 foot section in the center needs to be steamed.

The jig or mold is the final piece of equipment required. This usually consists of a wood block, around which the steamed stock is bent and held in place by means of a cloth or

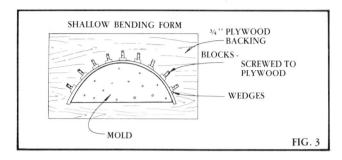

FIG. 3

metal strap, clamps, or post and wedges. Stock size and severity of the bend dictate the complexity of the jig. For gentle bends, the jig can consist of a mold block mounted on 3/4'' plywood with holding blocks every few inches along the outside radius. The stock is hand bent into position, then snugly fit in to place by means of wedges (Figure 3).

A jig for larger stock with a more severe bend requires a heavier mold block (preferably bolted to the floor) and a support strap with stop blocks at each end. If you have ever done any small scale bending, you know that most failures occur on the outside of the bend. In fact, wood compresses a lot more than it stretches. Consequently, the support strap is necessary. The stock is cut to fit between the stop blocks. As it

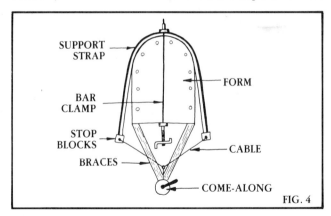

FIG. 4

is bent, the stop blocks prevent the wood from stretching and most of the cells are compressed. The support strap also holds the wood, keeping it from splitting and failing. The strap and stock is clamped in to place at the top of the form and pulled in to position by chain hoists, come-alongs or clamps (Figure 4).

Spring Back

When making any mold for steam bending, spring back must be taken into account. The amount of spring back depends on the species, thickness of stock, severity of the bend and the length of time the steamed stock is left in the jig. Even under ideal conditions, some spring back is inevitable. Consequently, the mold must be shaped so as to **over bend** to compensate for anticipated spring back. There is no formula for predicting spring back, only experience and trial and error. After the first piece is bent and removed from the jig, spring back is observed and the mold must be reshaped to compensate.

"...Beware of the steam coming from the box; it can cause second or third degree burns..."

One thing that seems to minimize spring back is the length of time the stock is left in the jig. I once left four sets of chair splats in the molds for about three weeks near the wood stove. When removed, they were down to less than 6% moisture content and had the smallest amount of spring back I have ever seen. This is not to say the bent stock must remain in the jig that long. Jigs are complex and expensive to make in multiples. Rather, drying jigs can be made once the bend has set, usually after about a day. A drying jig can be nothing more complex than a bar clamp holding the legs of a U-shaped bend together.

The Bending Process

After all of this preparation, the actual bending process is relatively straightforward. Make sure all stock is prepared and at hand. The boiler should have a good head of steam. Then load the stock in to the steam box. The time needed for proper steaming varies. Generally, the thicker (and dryer) the stock, the longer the steaming time. As a starting rule of thumb, for wood with a moisture content of 20%, try about one hour per one-half inch of thickness. Experience with specific species and bends should amend that to a more specific time for your operation.

Once the wood is ready, it should be taken out and immediately placed in the jig. Wear gloves. Beware of the steam coming from the box; it can cause second and third degree burns. You have only a couple of minutes to work, since the wood quickly cools and dries, losing its pliability. Often it helps to have someone else present to help hold, bend, and clamp. The sooner the stock is fully clamped and supported in the jig, the higher the chances of success.

Heat Bending

A slight variation of steam bending is heat bending. It is used by luthiers on guitars, dulcimers, and violin sides. Heat bending is much faster and easier, but can be used only on thin stock, up to one-fourth inch thick. The wood to be bent is merely forced over an electric heat bender, stove pipe, or cut off section of water pipe heated with a blow torch. The wood is forced back and forth and pulled into position. Water can be brushed on the inside of the bend to prevent scorching, but is not necessary if the heat iron is not too hot. The intense heat on the inside curve causes compression of the wood cells. The stock remains in its new shape upon cooling.

TABLE A
Bending Properties of Domestic Hardwoods

WOOD	PERCENT OF UNBROKEN PIECES
Ash	67
Basswood	2
Beech	75
Birch	72
Chestnut	56
Elm	74
Hackberry	94
Hickory	76
Maple, Hard	57
Maple, Soft	59
Oak, Red	86
Oak, White	91
Pecan	78
Sweet Gum	67
Sycamore	29
Walnut	78
Willow	73
Yellow Poplar	58

Source: U.S. Forest Products Lab. *Wood Handbook: Wood as An Engineering Material.*

TABLE B
Limiting Radii of Curvature (In Inches for One Inch Stock)

Wood	Supported by Strap	Unsupported by Strap
Ash	4.5	13.0
Beech	1.6	16.0
Birch, Yellow	3.0	17.0
Cherry	2.0	17.0
Douglas Fir	18.0	33.0
Elm, American	1.7	13.5
Hickory	1.8	15.0
Locust, Black	1.5	11.0
Oak, White	0.5	13.0
Oak, Red	1.0	11.5
Spruce, Sitka	36.0	32.0
Walnut	1.0	11.0

ABOUT THE AUTHOR:

Chris Becksvoort is a contributing editor to **The American Woodworker.** *He also operates his own woodworking business under the name of C.H. Voort in New Gloucester, Maine.*

Woodturning
Developing The Design

by Scott D. Emme

INTRODUCTION

Woodturning is one of the oldest power tool processes known to man and has evolved from a process used for producing necessities into one used for work considered by most, to be an art form. This same evolution, however, has not occurred in the consideration of design elements by many turners presently involved in this art. In this article, the goal is not to teach a specific aspect of turning itself, nor offer unique ideas for projects and turning techniques; rather, this is meant to be a basic guideline for the development of design for turning. Design considerations offered here are those that have worked well for me and perhaps can benefit other turning enthusiasts searching to achieve a better insight into their own woodturning designs.

Learning to design for turning should begin, as most learning processes begin, with observation and emulation of work already completed. Observation of professional works in turning, whether it be in gallery exhibits, craft shows, gift shops, or from the many books currently available on woodturning, is the best stepping stone for a turner attempting to develop his/her own taste and sense of design. Observation should not end here, however; designs for turning can be derived from other media as well, including pottery, glassware, and oddly enough, even nature. Pottery, especially American Indian pottery, has greatly influenced my own turning, specifically in its incorporation of subtle line and shape with the enhancement of geometrical patterns as the focal point which has much the same effect as segmented and mosaic turnings. Glassware often suggests ideas for the wood lathe, especially in the turning of goblets, and even more in the chip carving and shaping possibilities presented upon completion of the turning. Finally, nature itself can suggest wood turned shapes, since most living things and even a few nonliving are based on formal balance of symmetry. Nature does not necessarily offer the entire design in its finished form, though Steven Hogbin's table interpretation of a bird in flight *(Fine Woodworking #17)* is a dynamic example of observing what nature has to offer.

These are the major sources of my own ideas, and are by no means the complete list of possibilities for the observant woodturner to gain new ideas for his/her own wood lathe projects.

When a feature is added to the turning, such as the handle added to this ash coffee mug, the design is usually low, allowing emphasis to be given to the handle and the lid.

SKETCHBOOK

Observation is a marvelous tool but short memory is a definite hinderance to the incorporation of what we have observed into the actual work. Therefore, a sketchbook is invaluable in the design process. It should be considered the research library for design possibilities, and nothing should be considered too menial to warrant addition. Even notes with or without sketches for projects can be a beneficial entry. When the turner is looking for ideas and visits an art gallery or museum, the sketchbook should be a companion, and when a unique shape displays itself, the addition can be made immediately. Likewise, when thumbing through a magazine or watching television produces a new idea, sketches should be added for future reference. If the sketchbook is not available, it should not mean the thought cannot be recorded; even a napkin may save an idea for later addition into the sketchbook. There are times when the sketchbook may seem out of place, especially in fine art galleries or when walking through a gift shop or craft sale. Yet this should not deter the turner from the acquisition of a new idea. Simply fill in the sketchbook upon returning to the car or home. Another method I often use is to carry along a camera and photograph the ideas that stand out, since a camera seems less conspicuous than a sketchbook and just as useful in acquiring new ideas.

As time goes by, the sketchbook will begin to be an automatic response to a new idea. Once several entries have been made, design ideas will gradually begin to surface, and the design process is set into motion. The task of designing is not one to be made in haste nor should it be considered a mere formality of the turning process; rather, it should be an organized, carefully conceived aspect of the work itself. In my work, I have chosen a set of basic guidelines that, when followed, will produce the desired effect. These rules are quite obvious but are all too often overlooked by the individual who is ready to turn before knowing what the project should actually look like upon completion.

The two goblets shown above illustrate the use of different proportions to obtain the same end result.

FUNCTION

Quite possibly the foremost reason for beginning a project is the need for or the request for a specific item to be produced. This does not necessarily mean the piece is or is not a functional item, though most requests for projects seem to be function oriented. Function, when discussing turning, is a rather obscure term, since aesthetic quality is quite often the foremost (and in some cases) the only function of the wood-turned item. The turning, which fulfills no purpose other than aesthetics, even though a museum quality piece, will soon become lost in its surrouundings and be taken for granted when it is viewed every day by the same people, but never used. The truly functional, yet aesthetically appealing turning, is usually the most appreciated piece that can be produced. It not only caters to a need, it provides a warm decoration, and even more, a sense of fulfillment when an object designed and turned actually performs as anticipated.

PROPORTION

Proportion, which constitutes the feeling of stability within an object, is not a major concern for most turning projects, but for many, it can be the difference between a successful and unsuccessful result. Proportions for turning are rather ambiguous, but most turnings appear somewhat more stable when a proportion is established and used. The proportions I use for turning are usually whole, odd-numbered ratios, much the same as furniture and cabinet proportions. These can vary according to projects, and many projects can be made in more than one proportion and still have successful results. The proportions and their major projects as I use them are shown in the following chart:

Proportion	Project
1 : 8	serving tray, plate, and platter
3 : 8	table lamp, wine goblet, candle holder, and bowls
5 : 8	table lamp, wine goblet, candle holder, decanters and bowls
2 : 3	mugs, glasses, candle holder, and bowls
3 : 5	candle holder, mugs, glasses, and bowls

NOTE: Bowls can incorporate the proportion in either direction, i.e. a bowl can be categorized as a 3 : 5 proportion whether it is 10" diameter x 6" height or 6" height x 10" diameter.

The preceeding proportion chart may appear confusing, but it is actually quite simple to use. Once you have chosen the project to be turned, determine one of the major dimensions you wish to use: height or diameter. Decide what proportion is to be incorporated, according to the chart, and set up an algebraic equation to find the unknown dimension; as shown in the following examples. Remember, always place the largest dimension desired for your turning in the "bottom" position of the equation, whether it is the known or unknown dimension.

To find the dimensions of a table lamp to fit the 3 : 8 proportion:

EXAMPLE 1: Proportion = 3 : 8; Height = 18; Diameter = X

To solve: $\dfrac{3}{8} = \dfrac{X}{18}$ $3 \times 18 = 54$ $54 \div 8 = 6\tfrac{3}{4}$

ANSWER: The lamp should be 18" tall and 6¾" in diameter.

EXAMPLE 2: Proportion = 3 : 8; Height = 18; Diameter = X

To solve: $\dfrac{3}{8} = \dfrac{6}{X}$ $8 \times 6 = 48$ $48 \div 3 = 16$

ANSWER: The lamp should be 16" tall and 6" in diameter.

LINE AND SHAPE

Function and proportion play major roles in achieving the initial phase of designing a turning, but once the actual idea is conceived it is line and shape that must be foremost in the turner's mind. Line and shape essentially govern every characteristic of a turning's appearance, from the outlining shape or silhouette to the selection of the wood to be used, and every aspect can enhance or hinder the final appearance of the turning.

There are basically four cuts or forms of line and shape in a turner's repertoire: the cove, the bead, the "V" cut and the square shoulder. Using these cuts, or combinations and variations of these cuts, results in most every shape possible on the wood lathe. With these cuts in mind, the intensity of line and shape can be divided into two groups which I term high design and low design. High design incorporates the basic cuts as the focal point, or one of the major focal points, of the turning. These types of turnings are commonly of more aesthetic value than functional value, as exemplified by the ornate turning associated with furniture finials and candle holders. High design is characterized by a very prominent shape on the outline or silhouette of the turning which results in very distinct lines running around the turning separating these shapes. Low design, as the term implies, is a subtle type of turning in which the basic cuts forming line and shape are of secondary importance compared to other aspects of the turning. An example of low design includes the stretchers of a chair, in which the turning is meant to decorate but distract from the attention given to the overall appearance of the chair's other features. The incorporation of segmented turnings and inlays, which would lose some of their prominence if they were incorporated with high design, is another aspect of low design.

When a unique grain figure presents itself, as in the knot of this walnut bowl, the design should be low design.

Though the walnut/maple bowl and the walnut candleholder are both meant to be of aesthetical value in a room's decor, they obtain this value by incorporating opposite types of design. The candleholder is an example of high design, whereas the bowl uses low design to reach the same result—aesthetic enhancement.

Along with the turning's physical outline and purpose, there is another factor to consider when discussing line and shape: the lines and shape already present in the wood being used. The grain figure should influence the overall appearance of the finished turning. One of the joys I have discovered in turning is observing the unique configurations that result from an interesting grain figure when the various basic cuts are introduced. The resulting figure can be an overwhelming addition to the work, and to some degree, the turner can regulate the figure's final appearance if the proper attention is given during the work. For example, to achieve a circular grain figure on the tangential surface of the turning, a cove or bead should be cut. By controlling the size and shape of these cuts, the size and shape of the circular figure can likewise be controlled.

COLOR

Usually a woodturning will become a detail of a specific room's decor; therefore, it is very important that its features match or compliment its surroundings, especially in color. Color coordination has been a key to successful decoration for centuries, and though wood color is commonly thought of in terms of browns and cream colors, there are very bright, bold colors (ranging from the yellows of mulberry and osage orange, to the purple of amaranth and the red of padauk) available in the world of wood. Since turnings are details and relatively small features in the room decor, they may be used as color additives. Brightly colored woods, usually considered too gaudy for cabinetry, can be used quite effectively to compliment the existing colors of the room.

Color can be attained through the selection of woods, but wood may also have its color altered or even changed, with the vast array of stains, dyes, and tinting pigments available for attaining almost any color imaginable. In my work, and in my personal opinion, stains and dyes should be used only when a specific purpose requires it; otherwise, I prefer to leave wood in its own natural color. Among the purposes for staining wood, the most common are: 1) *Staining to match existing stained pieces,* especially if a turning is to sit upon a piece of furniture and is to match it as closely as possible; 2) *Staining to bring out grain figure,* most commonly to enhance the difference between early wood and late wood and the different special grain figures of wood, including burl, knots and crotch grain; and 3) *Staining to cover blemishes,* such as bleached spots or small patches of unwanted sapwood or dry rot which has discolored the wood. One final note on staining: never stain a turning that is to be used as a food container.

PUTTING IT ALL TOGETHER

As discussed, designing for turning is more than a mere formality of the work. Much observation, consideration, and a generous portion of trial and error must be used when deciding upon the appearance of a turned object. When actually designing the turning, the elements of design must be correlated so as to provide a project that can fulfill all its requirements, aesthetically as well as functionally. Correlation of these elements, however, will not be as simple as it first appears, for nothing in designing a turning is truly "clear cut." The turner must decide what function is being fulfilled and establish whether high design or low design would be more beneficial, which in turn, depends on whether or not segments, inlay, or carving is desired. Then when the turner has decided upon the turning's appearance and has completed the final sketch, he/she may choose a piece of stock with a certain figure or color that suggests a completely different design possibility, in which case, the process may have to begin all over again.

It seems an impossible task to arrive at a final design for a turning, yet with practice, observation, and good luck, the turner can begin to produce well designed turnings. Turnings, when finished, provide not only an eye pleasing piece that fits well into the environment, but they provide the turner with the joy and fulfillment of accomplishment that comes from the transformation of an idea (once recorded in a sketchbook) into the reality of an aesthetic, functional wood turned object.

Color and grain figure can quite often be all a turning needs to have its own distinction, as in this osage orange fruit bowl.

REFERENCES
Gibbia, S.W., *Wood Finishing and Refinishing,* Van Nostrand Reinhold Pub. Co.: New York, 1954.
Nish, Dale L., *Creative Woodturning,* Brigham Young University Press, Provo, Utah, 1976.
Nish, Dale L., *Artistic Woodturning,* Brigham Young University Press, Provo, Utah, 1980.
Hogbin, Steven, *Woodturning: The Purpose of the Object,* Van Nostrand Reinhold Pub. Co.: New York, 1980.

ABOUT THE AUTHOR:
Scott D. Emme is a woodworking instructor at Southeast of Saline High School in Gypsum, Kansas. He is also adjunct professor of industrial education at Fort Hays State University in Hays, Kansas.

Microwave Drying For Turning

by Scott D. Emme

Woodturning is an aspect of woodworking that is all too often overlooked by lumber yards and saw mills. As a result, it is rare to find turning stock large enough for a salad bowl or decorative lamp, and the woodturner usually resorts to the lamination of 4/4 and 8/4 stock to arrive at the required dimension. Today, however, technology has provided the woodturner a new tool without even realizing it; the microwave oven.

The microwave oven is fast becoming a common household appliance, and it is likely that most turners can gain access to one, even it if is for only one experimental attempt. The microwave, likewise, makes it possible to use stock that is free or at least inexpensive, since even pieces from a firewood pile can result in unique and beautiful turnings. One of the major drawbacks in using the microwave for drying stock to be turned is the question, "How do I do it?" The proceeding information is a basic outline of the microwave process from working the green stock to drying the stock to completing the dried stock on the lathe.

The first step is to obtain the stock to be turned. This particular step should become quite easy once you have done a little thinking and looking, and as many articles and books readily explain, wood is really rather commonplace when you want to find it; firewood, tree removal services, etc. Since obtaining wood for this process is hopefully no significant problem, and so many other writings contain more explicit information on how to find, cut, and treat green wood than this article will discuss, I will not expound upon the subject further, rather, I will restrict this discussion to the drying of green turnings.

With the wood supply in hand, it is time to consider what to do with your resource. First and foremost, the end grain of the stock should be sealed immediately upon cutting to prevent checking; paste wax, paint, and even glue will accomplish this task. Once cut and end coated, the stock should be allowed to begin the drying process on its own for one or two months, so place the stock in a cool, dry place at first. This step is not actually a requirement for successful drying in the microwave, but a microwave will dry the wood so rapidly, warping and checking may become a problem. Stock that has already become a little more stable and dry on its own, however, is likely to retain its original shape better. This wait may seem inconvenient, but with an ongoing search for wood, you will soon have a continuous supply of partially dried stock from which to choose.

ROUGHING THE STOCK

From the collection of drying stock, select the piece to be turned and decide which surface of the stock is to be trued for mounting on the lathe. Truing or surfacing of the stock can be accomplished with drawknife, hand plane,

PHOTOGRAPHS BY CRAIG COYLE

jointer, belt sander, or whatever method you can find that will produce a flat smooth surface for mounting the stock on the lathe. Bowls and turnings requiring a faceplate should be secured with screws, and for the sake of a process described later, care should be taken to align two of the screws on the same annual ring grain line.

The rough turning of green wood will be easier and more efficient if the stock is cut into a round shape on the band saw first. This however, may be impossible for turnings larger than the saw's capacity or for those who do not have a band saw, but this should not deter you from rounding the stock somewhat with hand saw, gouge, or even a chain saw. Regardless of the method or how crude the method may be, it is still easier and safer than placing a massive piece of square stock on the lathe and attempting to work on a machine with excessive vibration.

Splitting stock to be dried. Note that the ends have been sealed.

The photo above illustrates the three major stages of microwave drying. The blank on the left shows a piece that has been split to the desired rough size and the ends coated with wood glue. The cylinder on the right is a piece which has been mounted between centers and rough turned to 3½" in diameter, ends coated in paste wax and microwaved to 10% M.C. The bowl with lid pictured in the center is the final product of the walnut originally destined to become a fire.

If the turning is to be a bowl, the walls and bottom should be turned to about one inch in thickness and depth, as uniform as possible. If the project is not to be hollowed, such as a candleholder, then the turning should be one constant diameter its entire length and approximately ½ to ¾ inch larger than the largest finished diameter of the project. (NOTE: If you do not finish the rough turning process at one time, leaving even for a coffee break, wax the stock to prevent checks. Some woods will begin checking within minutes when exposed to the open air!) Upon completion of the rough turning process, apply a generous coat of paste wax to the entire turning; remove the stock from the faceplate and wax the bottom of the turning as well. (Do not use paint, resins, or glue for this step since you will not want these substances in your microwave.) The piece is now ready to dry. REMEMBER: MICROWAVES AND METAL DO NOT MIX—REMOVE THE FACEPLATE AND SCREWS!

Some woods will begin checking within minutes when exposed to air.

Before beginning the process discussion for microwave drying, one point should be made clear. There are several variables in this process which make it almost impossible to establish one clear cut method for all the green turnings you might attempt. Each type of wood, each different size of turning, each type of project, and each individual turning may react differently as it dries, therefore the method discussed here is the basis for starting the microwave drying process, and may require some modifications for other turnings. Experience, experimentation and possibly a failure or two will lead to the necessary modifications for your own successful drying in the microwave oven.

The bell pictured was turned from a 4 x 4 oak piece which was salvaged from a packing crate. The handle was turned separately from a walnut branch. The oak piece registered 18% M.C. when first checked, and required only one complete session in the microwave to obtain an 8% M.C. (3½x8).

DRYING THE STOCK

In any drying process there must be some basis for determining when the stock is dry. There are two basic methods that will be discussed here. First, a moisture meter may be used, and if a lot of microwave drying is to be undertaken, it may be worth the money to purchase one of the pocket meters on the market today. If a moisture meter is not available or not feasible, however, then the drying can be monitored with the weight method just as effectively.

MOISTURE METER PROCESS

When a moisture meter is available, simply place the waxed, rough turning in the microwave and run the oven for about two minutes on medium-low (defrost if your microwave is not adjustable). At the end of the two minutes, remove the turning and set it in the open air for two to three minutes. Repeat this process about ten times or twenty minutes in the oven. After the final time, the stock will be quite warm and the surface quite possibly moist, so set the turning aside and allow it to ''rest'' overnight. Check the moisture content with the meter. If it is 10% or less, the piece should be dry enough to turn with no significant problems. If, however, the moisture content is above 10%, place the turning back in the oven and repeat the drying process about five times or ten minutes in the oven. Allow the turning to ''rest'' overnight once again, then recheck the moisture content. The process may be repeated as needed, but I have yet to have a partially dried turning require more than three sessions in the microwave before finish turning.

WEIGHT PROCESS

The process without a meter begins by accurately weighing the stock and recording its weight; any scale that is accurate to within ounces will work, i.e. a postal scale or food scale. Place the stock in the microwave and run the oven on medium-low for two minutes. Again, remove the turning for two to three minutes between oven runs. Repeat the process ten times or twenty minutes in the oven and allow the turning to ''rest'' overnight. At this point, record the weight of the stock; note the weight loss thus far. Repeat the microwave process five additional times or ten minutes in the oven. Allow the stock to ''rest'' overnight, then record the weight once again. Now compare the weight of the turning after the first time in the oven with the weight after the second

Walnut hollow bowl with lid. Taken from a stack of firewood this piece measured 19% moisture at the beginning and required only one session in the microwave to reach 12% M.C. (3½x6D)

time in the oven. If they are the same or at least within a couple of ounces, the turning should be stable and dry enough to finish turn. Repeat the oven and weighing process as needed until the weight of the turning has stabilized.

FINISH TURNING

Upon completion of the drying process, the stock is ready to be finish turned, but two minor problems will need to be dealt with before work can actually begin. First, it will be evident that during the drying process some shrinkage occurred across the grain of the stock, but little if any occurred with the grain. This shrinkage will likely have distorted the base to the degree that it will require truing with a plane or belt sander before remounting on the faceplate. Secondly, the distortion from drying will have moved the faceplate screws out of alignment. As mentioned earlier, two screws should have originally been placed on the same grain line, and because the wood moved little if any in length, these two screws should still be aligned with the faceplate for remounting. Install the two screws that have their pilot holes aligned with the faceplate, then redrill the pilot holes for the other two screws as needed for their installation.

Once the stock is remounted on the faceplate, caution should be taken to treat the stock as a rough turning. The distortion that took place during the drying process will require reshaping which, if done in haste, will reduce the wall thickness to a degree that may interfere with the various shapes and designs that were desired on the project. Once the turning is again spinning round and smooth, the turning can be cut to its desired shape and appearance, sanded and finished just as if you had been fortunate enough to find a large, dry piece of stock for your turning project.

REFERENCES:

Nish, Dale L., *Artistic Woodturning,* Brigham Young University Press, Provo, Utah, 1980.

Stirt, Al, *Green Bowls, Fine Woodworking,* issue #3, (Summer 1976), pp. 37-39.

ABOUT THE AUTHOR:
Scott D. Emme is a woodworker/teacher in Gypsum, Kansas. He also wrote "Developing The Design" in **The American Woodworker,** *Dec., 1985.*

DRYING IN THE ROUND

by B. William Bigelow

One fine fall day, while lying on the wood pile listening to the beetles chew the oak beneath me, the idea came to me of drying wood in the round. But before any readers jump to unreasonable conclusions here, it must be said in my defense that I was resting from splitting an enormous pile of wood (well, at least a respectable pile). With the body uncomfortably resting and sleep out of the question, my mind returned to woodworking. How could I make a bird house, canister, planter, jewelry box, and a bud vase out of that chunk of green butternut that was so uncomfortably levering my back out of position? Within four weeks, with the addition of several scraps of flat stock, it was done! The process of cutting and drying green cylinders, described here, I will call drying in the round.

Often as a beginning woodturner, I have practiced on green stock from the wood pile (green wood being defined as any wood above the fiber saturation point). When turning green wood, cool shavings fly, producing a turning which is smooth and gleaming as if it were finished. If only it would last. Within minutes the wet wood evaporates its finish and hours later, deep checks develop. Checks, enlarging into cracks, are the result of the wood relieving itself of stress, generated by uneven shrinkage during drying.

It was this checking, radially increasing from the center, that first prompted me to core a round branch section and observe what happens when the outside cylinder dries. The first cylinders were cut on the lathe, mounted with the end grain attached to a face plate. The round section was turned outside with a tail stock support and then cut inside as deeply as possible and finally parted so that only a cylinder with both ends removed remained. The end grain of the cylinders was sealed and then set aside to dry. When dry, I turned

the cylinders as I would in a glued up stave construction.

The process of cutting cylinders on the lathe has limited advantages. Cylinders can be made seamless for special canisters or clock frames. It is, however, quite laborious and wasteful of stock. Later, I developed ways of cutting multiple cylinders from the same log section using the band saw and settling for one glued seam.

I have experimented with many native hardwoods, including butternut, red oak, sumac, apple wood, black cherry, and birch with equal success. The cylinders dry quickly, without cracking, in about a month. The drying time will, of course, vary, depending on relative humidity, temperature, air circulation, wall thickness and species. The cylinders are weighed after cutting and periodically thereafter. When the weight of the cylinder stabilizes, it has reached equilibrium moisture content (EMC) and can be used. Final drying should occur in the same type of environment as that in which the wood will be used, just as you would when working with flat stock.

The cylinders can be cut from any non resinous wood that has not cracked. With a little practice, it will take less than ten minutes to cut and glue each cylinder, and therefore it will be easy to build up a stock for future use. I have made canisters, clock frames, wall sconces, planters, mail boxes, bread trays, lamps, jewelry boxes, bud vases, and many parts for larger pieces from these cheap and inexpensive sources of round stock (the only doubting skeptic here is my wife, who believes that I can't finish anything in a month!). All that is required is green stock, a sturdy band saw, glue and a clamping arrangement.

The maximum height and width of each cylinder is limited by the capacity of the band saw. As the round stock is placed upright on the band saw table, the maximum length of each cylinder is limited by the cutting height capacity of the band saw. I frequently start with a large cylinder 11″ long and up to a foot in diameter cut on a 20″ Powermatic. It is best, however, to experiment with cutting techniques on smaller stock. Small underpowered three wheeled band saws with their thin blades are not equal to the task.

Choose green stock as round as possible with the pith centered. This is important if the cylinder is to be eventually turned on the lathe and you want the cylinder to dry round. Stay away from resinous woods that will gum up everything, including you. Square the ends so the stock sits upright on the band saw table without rocking. I use a V-block with a mitre gauge for this purpose. (Figure 2). On the top end with a compass, draw the largest circle possible inside the bark layer. Using the same center, draw a second circle inside the first. (Figure 3). The wall thickness between the circles may vary with the intended use of the cylinder. After some research on the different radial and tangential shrinkage, I usually settle for half inch wall thickness (which is by happy coincidence the easiest fraction a tired woodworker can find! One half-inch wall thickness doesn't take long to dry and is plenty of stock to true up on the lathe for most applications. Continue to draw smaller circles until the minimum curve the band saw blade will negotiate is reached.

The band saw will be cutting to the maximum of its capacity and all adjustments should be checked. The guide blocks or bearings and the blade tension should be accurately adjusted. A dull blade with poor tooth set will only frustrate attempts to cut the cylinder, so this may be prime time for that new blade. I prefer a ¼″ skip tooth blade to negotiate the curves. The table should be freshy waxed and set at 90 degrees to the blade. The stock will rotate on the table during the cut, and a rough, or sticky table will ruin your accuracy.

Position the stock upright on the band saw table on the side of the blade comfortable to handle and with the circles in view. The easiest way to enter each circle is a straight tangent line. This, however, produces problems in gluing

FIGURE 2. Cross cutting the tree section.

as the scarf line tends to slide by under clamping. The solution is to enter each circle circumference more as a radius line and then swing to a tangent line, resulting in a slightly concave entry cut which will ease clamping problems. (Figure 4). A little experimentation will soon yield good results. Cut with one hand midway up the cylinder and use a push stick midway up nearest the blade. (Figure 5). Using a push stick nearest the blade will give good control and eliminate the danger if the blade suddenly exits.

Enter the stock into the first circle, carefully cut around until the entry point is past, then shut the band saw down and back the blade out. In some woods, the saw kerf must be gently pried apart to facilitate blade removal. Once the stock is free of the blade, slide the outside cylinder off. (Figure 6). Typically, I will cut two or three cylinders after the bark cylinder is cut. (Figure 7) Glue and save the outside bark cylinder as they make excellent birdhouses. I soak the core in water until I can cut a bud vase on the lathe. Right after the bud vase is cut, it must be drilled all the way through its center so it will dry without checking. After drying, the hole is plugged. (My woodstove is facing starvation.)

FIGURE 3. Drawing circles.

47

fter the cylinders are cut they must be glued. Cylinders that are left overnight will move so much that forcing the kerf line back will usually result in cracking. With some experimentation, I have found large stainless steel worm clamps the easiest clamping method; however, strap clamps, heavy elastics, or inner tube rubber will also work. I had reservations about using water based yellow glue (alphatic resion) on the green wood, but it has worked just fine. Glue the saw kerf lines working the glue in with a piece of stiff cardboard and then clamp. *(Figure 8)*. Next, coat the end grains of the cylinder with sealer (I use glue here, also) to prevent end grain checking. Weigh each cylinder and record its weight on the cylinder wall with the date it was cut. *(Figure 9)*.

The circumference of the cylinder will change quickly as the wood loses moisture. Steel clamps that were applied tightly will slide off with finger pressure the next day. I have returned after two days to find the clamps had fallen off the cylinders!

Drying time will vary considerably depending on relative humidity, temperature, wall thickness, air circulation and

FIGURE 5.

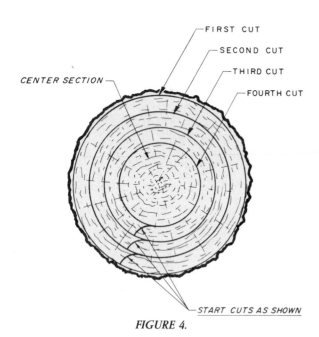

FIGURE 4.

FIGURE 6. Slide outside cylinder off.

species. The cylinders are safe to use when they reach equilibrium moisture content with the surrounding air. Continue weighing the cylinders periodically, and when the weight stabilizes, they are safe to use. Final drying should take place in the same type of environment in which the cylinder will eventually be used, especially if the cylinder will be glued to a bottom which restricts further movement, as in a canister set.

One advantage of drying in the round is no stickers are required. I rope the cylinders overhead out of the way where the air is warm, or sometimes I lay them sideways on a shelf and stack them like a wine rack (an idea for another project). With such a cheap supply of native hardwood from the

FIGURE 7. Cut stock.

firewood pile or an occasional blown down branch, I constantly find new ways of using these cylinders. This is also the easiest way to use hard wood species such as the fruit trees which are not normally sawn for reasonable prices. Unfortunately, I have not found a market for round wooden stove pipe, but who knows?

FIGURE 8. Gluing cylinders.

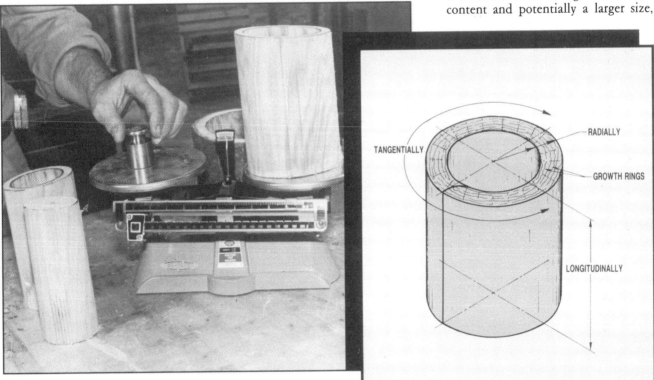

FIGURE 9. Weigh each cylinder and record the date and weight.

As green wood loses moisture and drops below the fiber saturation point, dimensional changes begin to take place. Wood will decrease in size as it moves from fiber saturation point (for many species around 30%) to oven dry. Wood will eventually reach a point somewhere between oven dry and fiber saturation point and stabilize at equilibrium with the surrounding air (EMC). Moisture content (MC) of the wood will slowly continue to adjust with the seasonal changes in humidity. To complicate things a bit, the wood does not lose moisture at the same even rate to its core, nor does it change in the same amount its shape in all directions. Most woods will decrease in size during drying about twice as much around the growth rings (tangentially) as they will across the growth rings toward the center of the tree (radially). The shrinkage along the length of the tree (longitudinally) is not nearly as great *(Figure 10)*. Also, as a sample is drying, the moisture content in different parts will not always be the same. The outside of the wood and the area near the end grain will dry faster as moisture travels much faster toward the end grain than any other direction. As the outside of the wood dries, leaving the inside with a higher moisture content and potentially a larger size,

FIGURE 10.

stresses develop. These stresses, coupled with the stress of the difference between radial and tangential movement, produce the cracks, warp, twists, and cup. Wood, being hydroscopic, will to some extent take on water with high humidity and reverse these changes. Woodworkers try to work with stock which has reached equilibrium moisture content and anticipate the changes that will take place during seasonal changes of humidity. Today, with our central heating systems, we anticipate greater dimensional changes than earlier cabinetmakers had to allow for.

When green cylinders are cut, glued, and allowed to dry, they will shrink without cracking, because their shape allows them to move and relieve the drying dimensional changes. The greatest tangential shrinkage around the growth rings can be measured as the decrease of the circumference of the cylinder. The radial shrinkage (which is about half of the tangential change) can be measured by the decrease of the thickness of the cylinder wall. The smallest change is longitudinal and will affect the length of the cylinder. If the cylinder wall is thin enough (depending on species, but usually less than one inch) and if the end grain is sealed, all three dimensional changes will be relatively independent. The circumference of the cylinder (now without its core) can move independently. The wall thickness and the length of the cylinder can also change its size without restriction. A cylinder without knots will not crack as it dries. It is interesting to note that a cylinder cut with a knot in the side wall will usually check around the knot, exactly as the round stock will check and crack if cylinders had not been cut out of it.

I experimented with black cherry and butternut to measure the tangential change of the cylinders during the drying cycle. The circumference of the cylinders was measured after gluing and when the cylinders were at equilibrium with the surrounding air. Lacking a moisture meter, I weighed the cylinders, and when the weight stabilized, I determined they were at EMC. The moisture content of the cylinders was calculated from the average relative humidity of the shop. Average humidity during the 30 day test (20 samples) was at 28%, and the final moisture content was calculated to be at 5-7%. The chart in Figure 11 illustrates how the wood dries in relation to time. The black cherry changed 5.4% from fiber saturation point to about 6% MC. The tangential change in the butternut under the same conditions was 4.9%.

An excellent resource is *Understanding Wood,* Bruce Hoadley, Taunton Press.

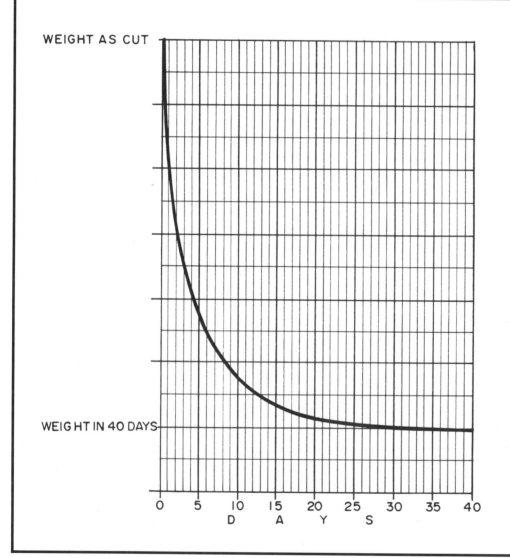

FIGURE 11.

ABOUT THE AUTHOR:
B. William Bigelow is a cabinetmaker/writer. He also teaches woodworking at Conual High School in New Hampshire.

How To Inlay

by Allan E. Fitchett

An inlay may be used to decorate the surface of an object, such as a piece of furniture, by inserting a design, often referred to as an inlay or marquetry assembly, into a grooved or recessed area.

Inlay is an ancient art/craft which can be traced back to the early Egyptians. The pharoahs and kings of that era would compete to obtain the finest craftsman to design and construct their furniture and rooms, embellishing them with intricate inlay designs.

The materials used for inlay can be wood, copper, brass, gold, silver, aluminum, tortoise shell, ivory, horn, bone, pearl, plastic, etc. The tools used for inlaying a design can range from a hammer and chisel to the small hand router plane, large hand router plane, electric router, electric laminate trimmer, drill press and the most modern technique—the laser beam. The use of the router plane and the electric router are the techniques discussed in this article.

Modern commercially-made inlays are made up of various types of veneer to form the design. This design is usually surrounded by a piece of veneer referred to as a "waster" (Fig. 1), which is used to keep all of the small pieces of veneer which make up the design in place. One side of this assembly is usually covered with paper or gummed tape which also assists in keeping the design in place. The paper or gummed taped side of the assembly is the final or face side of the assembly and this paper or tape should remain in place until the assembly has been inlaid and glued into place and the adhesive used is allowed to dry properly.

Once you have selected your inlay, it now becomes necessary to provide a recessed area in the surface into which you will insert your inlay. The following steps may assist you in your endeavors.

No.1—If your selected inlay is surrounded in a waster, it is now time to cut away the waste veneer from the inlay design. Use a craft knife with a #11 blade and carefully cut away the waste material (Fig. 2). Cut on a scrap piece of wood with the paper or taped side of the assembly down. Make many light passes with the knife, rather than trying to cut through in one or two passes of the knife, which is apt to crack the veneer or give you a rough edge.

No.2—Use a sharp pencil (no ink) and outline the position of your inlay on the surface where you are going to insert the inlay; remember the paper or taped side of the assembly is the face side, so keep this side of the assembly up (Fig. 3). Now check your penciled outline to be sure the position is correct. If not, erase the pencil mark and re-outline until the position is satisfactory to you.

No.3—When you have established the exact position for the inlay, use a few small pieces of masking tape and hold the inlay onto the surface. Again using the point of your craft knife with the #11 blade, scribe a light line into the surface, tracing carefully around the edge of the inlay (Fig. 4). As you cut through the small pieces of holding tape, replace them with new or additional pieces of tape so that the inlay does not move until you have completed the scribed outline onto the surface to be inlayed.

No.4—Remove the tape and inlay. With the craft knife, retrace the scribed outline on the surface, cutting down to

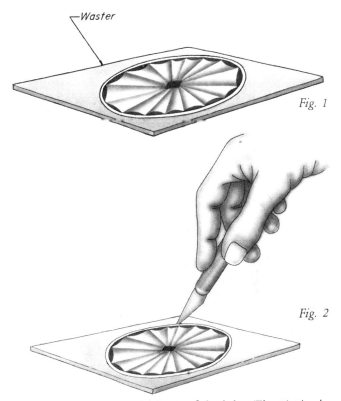

Waster

Fig. 1

Fig. 2

a depth equal to the thickness of the inlay (Fig. 5). Again, many light passes of the knife will produce a more accurate cut than one or two heavy passes.

No.5—If you elect to use an electric router or laminate trimmer to route out the inside area of your scribed outline, first use a 1/16″ straight fluted bit for your router. Set the bit to cut the depth or thickness of the inlay assembly. Carefully guide the router freehand to cut about 1/16″ inside the scribed outline. When this routed outline is complete, put in a ¼″ or larger router bit into the router or trimmer, set to cut the thickness of the inlay and proceed to remove the wood remaining inside the previous routed outline.

No.6—The 1/16″ strip remaining between the scribed outline and the routed-out area can now easily be removed by holding your craft knife on its side and carefully cutting along the bottom of the routed-out surface towards the original scribed outline. When this is complete, your inlay should fit perfectly into the routed recessed area.

No.7—The use of hand-held router planes may be slower than using an electric router, but excellent results can be obtained with this tool if you exercise patience and care. The use of the small Stanley #271 router plane is ideal for routing small areas (Fig. 6). Your hands can rest upon the surface and you can push or pull the tool using only your fingers, which provide superior control over the movement of the tool. If you use a hand router, it is suggested that you make several passes of the cutter, lowering the cutter each time until you have reached the final required depth. Move the router from the center of the area to be routed toward the scribed outline. After all of the area has been routed out, set the inlay in place to check for final fit.

No.8—To bond the inlay in place, do NOT use a contact type of adhesive. The use of Titebond or a similar type of adhesive is recommended. Apply a light coat of the adhesive to the side of the inlay assembly to be bonded plus a light coat of glue to the recessed area that you routed out. Insert the inlay assembly into the recessed area; press firmly using a veneer roller. Immediately wipe off any excess glue using a cloth dampened, not soaked, with water. Place a sheet of waxed paper or thin plastic over the inlaid area followed by six or eight sheets of newspaper. Place a board over the assembly and clamp the entire assembly and leave overnight. The next day, remove the clamps, paper, and plastic. Use a damp cloth and dampen the paper or gummed tape on the face side of the inlay. Use a blunt edged tool such as a putty knife and scrape away the paper or gummed tape. Be careful not to gouge the inlay or surrounding area.

No.9—Erase any pencil marks, then lightly sand the entire surface and prepare it for your favorite finish, varnish, lacquer or polyurethane. Your finished piece will be a unique masterpiece and will be a source of many compliments and much conversation.

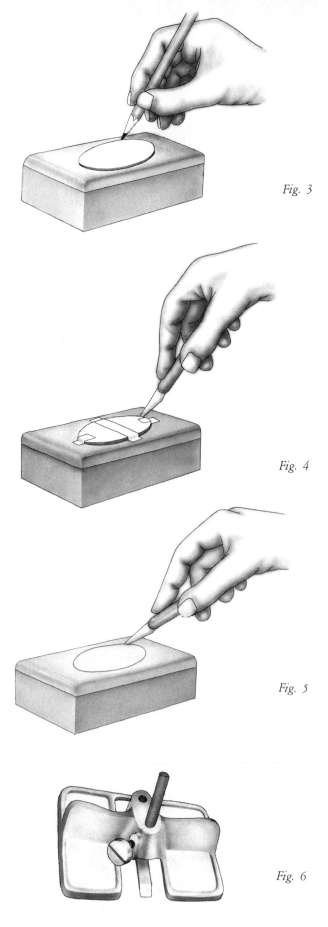

Fig. 3

Fig. 4

Fig. 5

Fig. 6

Illustrations by Jennifer Chiles

Helpful Hints

When using any type of router, it is most important that at least half the base of the router be in firm contact with the surface being routed. When routing large areas, it may be necessary to do it in sections, working from the center toward the outside so that you have a good portion of the router base in contact with the final surface at all times.

To set a router to cut the proper depth, simply place the piece to be inlaid under the base of the router away from the bit and then lower the bit to the surface. The bit then can only cut the thickness for which it has been set. If you use a hand router plane, select several sheets of paper until you have a pad the even thickness of the inlay. You can set the cutter to take shallower cuts by removing several sheets of paper from the pad and placing them under the base of the router plane. Gradually increase the sheets in the pad and place them under the base of the router plane, reset the cutter and make your cuts. Repeat this procedure until you have the original pad to set your cutter for the final cut. The use of sharp cutters is a must.

If you use an electric router, you can remove the base that is supplied by the manufacturer and replace it with a piece of ¼" clear plastic that has been cut away to give you a clear view of the tip of the router bit plus any scribed line or outlines on the surface. A large piece of plastic will also give you more stability on the surface being routed. Plastic is easily cut and formed using simple woodworking tools.

Commercially made inlays are available in many designs together with a wide variety of exotic and fancy border strips for inlaying. Border strips are easily inlaid by selecting a router bit to match the width of the border. Set the depth of the router bit, pass the router along a straight edge in proper relative position, and you are ready to glue in your border strip. A router bit leaves rounded edges; use your craft knife to square off any rounded edges if necessary. The use of straight fluted, sharp router bits is a must if using electric routers or laminate trimmers.

About The Author:

*Allan E. Fitchett is a professional restorer of antiques, a lecturer and an experienced marquetarian. He is a consultant to Albert Constantine and Son, Inc. of New York and has served as president of the Marquetry Society of America. He is co-author of **Modern Marquetry Handbook**.*

The Art Of Mother-Of-Pearl Inlay

By Tom and Mary Morgan

For many years mother-of-pearl and abalone shells have been used to enhance the beauty of musical instruments and furniture. These shells are considered to be art objects in their polished form. They are also used to make jewelry. The mother-of-pearl is white in color and the abalone is delicately colored shell of the palest blue, pink, purple and green. The industry went through a period when mechanization held the upper hand. There is presently a groundswell of activity of ornamentation in customizing guitars, mandolins and banjos that is practical as an art today.

There has always been an aura of mystery attached to the craft, when in fact, the necessary steps to achieve professional results are remarkably easy:

1) Start with the shape you have in mind, or the pattern you have chosen to duplicate.

2) Transfer this design to the piece of shell you have decided to use, by either drawing the outline on the shell or by glueing a paper pattern on the pearl.

3) Cut out the piece to be inlaid, and trim any rough edges.

4) Rout a hole that the pieces will fit into.

5) "Bed in" with Epoxe glue and a colored filler.

6) Sand off the glue/filler and enjoy!

The simplest application of the above is a round 'dot' with a matching drill bit to make the hole, and if everything has been properly matched up, virtually any type glue will give perfect results. The opposite end of the possibilities are very elaborate inlay patterns, like the 'Tree of Life' design used on some muscial instrument fingerboards, as well as engraved pearl inlays, which require an entirely separate set of tools and skills.

Nothing can add beauty and improve the value of a well-built stringed instrument more than to add delicate, tasteful and finely executed inlays of white tropical oyster or abalone shell, inset and sanded or polished to the desired degree. Shell from salt water has always been our choice of material, due to the greater lustre over fresh water mussels. All the long-established instrument companies (who set our 'role model' standards) have followed this guideline, without exception.

The choice of which materials are suitable for inlays is virtually unlimited, even though the bulk of our work has been in pearl, on stringed instruments. Anything that will contrast is possible, including snail shell, fresh water mussels, gold or silver wire, dark wood versus light woods, etc. For a customer who brought us a rifle stock to customize, we inlayed a delicate pearl heart into an ebony diamond, which in turn was set into the walnut stock for a 3-way contrast.

In furniture, contrasting woods may be used in either solid or veneer forms, and mother-of-pearl in many cases will enhance the beauty of the piece. Hopefully, this article will also be helpful in cases where existing furniture with missing inlay pieces can be successfully restored.

Example of the five steps to inlay. Pattern, draw around, relieve, glue in, sand off.

One unusual effect that was popular around the turn of the century occurred when musical instrument guard plates were made of real or celluloid simulated tortoise shell, with elaborate pearl, snail or abalone set therein. Refreshingly, a replication of period instrument appointments is still being done by the Custom Order Department of the C. F. Martin Guitar Company in Nazareth, Pennsylvania, which has one of the most respected inlay specialists in the business.

For less intricate shapes where a large number of the same piece is used, a thin metal template can be used to draw the pattern directly on the pearl, and the cutting can be done with carborundum 'cut-off' discs or steel saws in a Dremel Moto-Tool. We've always used the #280 tool, since it can be switched on and off with one hand, but a #380 with variable speeds would have an advantage in some applications, as in celluloid or plastic where the higher speed melts the material, rather than cut.

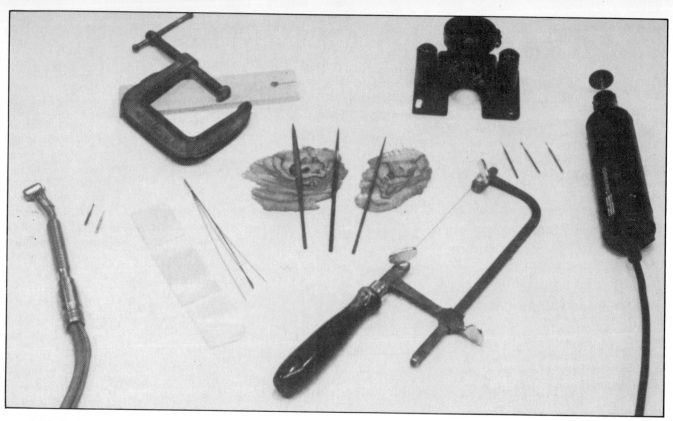

Useful inlaying tools: No. 280 Moto Tool w/cut off disc, engraving cutters and No. 229 base. Jeweler's saw frame and blades. Shell blanks and needle files. Sawing board and clamp. Dental drill and burrs (could use flexible shaft instead).

Virtually any hobby shop we've ever entered has had the Dremel tools and accessories in stock, but the Company has been a mainstay in our work, and by writing Dremel Manufacturing, 4915 21st Street, Racine, Wisconsin 53406 - telephone 414-554-1390, you can receive a handy reference list of what they have to offer. In our case, we've often had the #280 tools rebuilt after long and steady usage, and they provide a very reliable service here also, at a moderate cost.

We started our inlayings, many years ago, using a hand-held Moto-Tool, but for the last several years have been fortunate enough to acquire a surplus dental air drill (a much more expensive and efficient piece of equipment). For someone just starting, the Model #232 drill with handpiece and flexible shaft might be a logical alternative. For comparison sake, the #280 is rated at 30,000 r.p.m., their flexible shaft, 25,000, and a dental air drill 300,000! It is likely that other makes of flexible shafts, with heavier motors, would run too slow to be effective for this type work, and it is also not known whether the dental and Dremel cutter shafts will fit.

A more efficient method for cutting out more intricate and delicate shapes is to use the jeweler's saw, with its ultra-thin blades. The handle and blades are available from jeweler's supply houses (or the two instrument builders suppliers listed at the end of this article), and for most of the shapes we cut, the #1 blade works well.

The support you'll need is a thin piece of wood with a hole drilled (see photo) and a slot sawn to accomodate the blade. Clamp this board to the edge of your work bench, and be sure the teeth of the saw blade are set to cut on the down stroke. It will take a bit of practice to adjust the tautness to be tight enough, yet not break the blades.

Trimming pearl with Moto-tool in front of squirrel-cage fan.

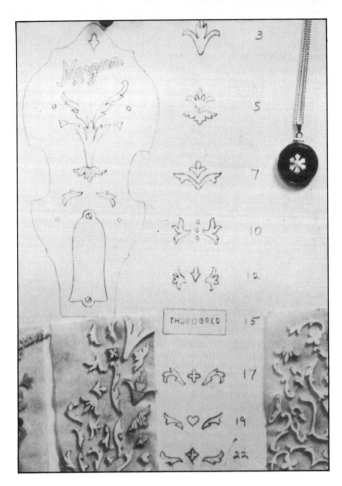

Morgan banjo layout sketch, with pearl pieces awaiting inletting. Necklace is a silver coin mounting with ebony insert and Martin guitar 'snowflake'.

Another area where caution is required, is holding and cutting the pearl without cutting your fingers. To gain some practice, one should start with larger blank pieces of pearl, with small patterns, using thumb and forefinger (or any combination of two fingers, with the blade to work between), and applying firm downward pressure to prevent the pearl jumping on the upward stroke. Saw with smooth, long strokes, always being careful to keep the blade exactly vertical. This will insure nice, square edges on the pieces you end up with, and although you should probably practice on simpler patterns, as your skills improve, there is virtually no limit to how intricate the final results can be.

The saw blade cuts approximately the same width as a pencil line, and it works well to saw directly on the line to cut down on the trimming or filing that is usually needed next. Simple needle files can be used to smooth the edges, although there are several items listed in the dental supply catalog, including stones and even diamond abrasives that are very efficient for trimming. The #1 blade will actually cut and turn within a space of approximately 1/64 of an inch (small enough for most of the 'corners' you'll need to cut into) and the secret is to turn the workpiece as you saw. For even finer detail, back the saw into a tight cut and saw out, or make separate cuts in from either side.

In some patterns, the pieces are mirror images, and especially with thinner 40 thousandths pearl, it is practical to saw two pieces glued together to insure a perfect match. Some attractive pearl inlay and wood marquetry have contrasting colors, and sometimes it is possible to saw two pieces at once

to give an 'instant' fit. In some guitars, a nice effect has been achieved by inlaying ebony blocks into a rosewood fingerboard, and then setting pearl designs into ebony. A nice effect is also achieved by using rectangles of white pearl with a triangle of abalone set into one edge.

Once the desired pieces are ready, the next step is to do an accurate layout on the material to be inletted. Our method, simply, is to position each piece, and hold it down with a small dowel sharpened like a pencil (with a blunt point to prevent slipping), and using a #3 pencil, an easy-to-follow outline is achieved. An alternate method is to glue the pearl with a very small amount of super glue, Duco cement or white glue, and then use the appropriate solvent to remove it. When using the glued-down method, you must use caution in getting the pieces loose (especially the narrower ones) as they can be easily broken. Some even choose to use a contrasting spray paint, working straight down to avoid a shadow effect, to show the exact shape to relieve, but you should use the method that works best for you.

To actually cut the hole, choose the smallest available burr and follow the *inside* of the lines, much like you would sketch on paper. For the Moto Tool, or flexible shaft and handpiece, a Dremel #108 engraving cutter of a #33½ dental burr (both of which are shaped like a truncated cone) will work well for the outline. Then switch to a larger burr of the same type to remove the rest. The reason for not using a round cutter here is to have the walls square (or even undercut) and not have a radius in the corners to stop the piece. In the past, dental burrs were made of high speed steel and carbide, and for our purpose, the carbides are much preferred. Modern burrs are all carbides, and even the ones your friendly dentist is ready to discard will still have a lot of use left in them for inlaying into wood. The cost, however, is not excessive, and you may want to start your project with new burrs instead.

Some inlay specialists prefer a #111 Dremel engraving cutter, in conjunction with one of the router bases made by Dremel, and this has the advantage of giving an even depth. There are small drawbacks, such as less delicate corners, and some difficulty in getting a light positioned so as to see the outlines. David Nichols (Custom Pearl Inlay, 1 Nell Manor Drive, Waddington, NY 13694) is a source of a much more exotic tool bit for routing with a base, though by comparison, the price is high, and we still prefer to do the relieving freehand.

By relieving inside the lines, you can gradually work toward the most nearly perfect fit, and with practice, you can see where your first outline cuts should be made. Proceed very slowly here, with very light enlarging cuts, and try the pearl piece often. Sometimes, it helps to erase any remaining pencil marks at this point, and as one side of the piece starts to fit into the hole, use the pencil again to show where it has to be relieved to accomodate the pearl. You should also guard against too tight a fit here, as the pearl still has to come out one last time for glueing, and could break if it gets wedged in.

The optimum now is to leave the pearl a few thousandths higher than the wood, as it can easily be sanded flush. Special care must be taken so that none of the corners are lower than the wood, but you can use scraps of sandpaper, masking tape, etc., as glued-in shim stock *in the bottom* of the hole, as the pearl and filler will hide any extraneous material. The next step is to mix a fine, matching wood dust (or commercially available filler) in a two-part Epoxe glue, and we prefer to use the slow variety to let one batch of mix do even elaborate jobs, once everything is in readiness. The 5-minute variety is very useful for smaller jobs, and when a faster end-product is desired.

Trimming a 'snowflake' with the Moto Tool.

By filling the holes with the mix, the pieces are carefully pushed in *level*, leaving plenty of excess squeezed out so there is less danger of gaps in the filler, and the dried material is relatively easy to sand off. We know at least one specialist who uses only clear Epoxe with no filler (the glue picks up the color of the surrounding wood), but it requires very accurate inletting, and would be a logical goal for the novice to strive for.

Once the filler/glue is completely dry, the only remaining step is to sand the inlaid part with the surrounding area flush, and the safest way to do this is to use a sanding block. We prefer 100 grit paper at this stage, and you'll need to use a light, slow stroke to cut fast and still keep the paper from loading up. A periodic, sharp rap against the workbench helps clear the sandpaper, and cleaning the paper with a wire brush is sometimes required.

After all the wood, filler and pearl is completely level, you should change to finer grades of sandpaper, but you'll be surprised how fast professional results will be achieved. For our work on instruments, we don't strive for a highly-polished look such as you would find on jewelry, compacts, and the like, because it has not been traditional to do so.

The supposition that pearl dust is especially hazardous probably goes back to the time when shell products were soaked in a poisonous solution to make them easier to cut. However, as with other dusts which should be avoided, it would be logical to wear some sort of mask for protection. When cutting and smoothing pearl edges with either the Dremel or dentist drill, we work in front of a small squirrel-cage fan that effectively pulls in the dust and carries it away from the person doing the work, but in the case of small, hard-to-hold pieces, it has sometimes also carried away the workpiece, never to be seen again!

There is a difference in the way some brands of Epoxe react, both on unfinished wood and also under lacquer or varnish finishes, the problem being that some brands show an unnatural shiny appearance or swell, with time. A known brand that we prefer is 'Sig' but may not be available at your hobby or hardware store, although the Sig Manufacturing Company, Inc., Montezuma, Iowa 50171, would likely welcome inquiries from you or your local dealer.

To touch briefly on the subject of engraving pearl, it can be as simple as taking a blank to your local jeweler, and having any of his available pantograph patterns followed. The material is not nearly as fragile or hard to work with as some would have you believe, and you can expect excellent results if it can be held firmly on the flat surface of the engraver table, and the cutting bit is small enough and sharp enough for the desired line weight.

Also, if you determine the ratio preferred on any given machine, and the style of follower used, one can make their own plexiglas patterns. For example, to duplicate a hand-engraved effect of a 1930's Gibson MASTERTONE banjo block, we photographed an original and made a 5:1 pattern, and in this way achieved a period appearance in a brand new piece. The 'grooves' cut into the pearl are then filled with jeweler's wax, India ink, or black lacquer, as the finishing step.

Hand engraved mother-of-pearl is a completely separate art form, requiring different tools and skills, and giving a different aesthetic effect. A good example would be a dragon made with a single or multiple pieces of flat shell, set in the wood as in the previous examples, but with very elaborate engraved detail often seen in oriental art. For all the intricacy displayed, the principle is simply to hand-cut varying weight and depth lines into the surface of the inlaid pieces with a variety of shapes and gravers. This is best done after the pearl has been set into the wood, and everything is perfectly level.

A corresponding example would be the elaborate engraving done on some of the metal work of banjos, mandolin and guitar machines and hardware, and especially firearms, where the waterfowl or upland game scenes help personalize the piece for its owner, as well as dictate how high the initial cost and collectors appreciation value will go.

Some instrument makers in this country have favored engraved pearl (Fairbanks and Vega to name two), but our efforts have been directed to other makes and non-engraved styles. There have been occasions to touch up areas that have either been worn or sanded off, and by breaking off the cutting portion of one of the smallest dental burrs and grinding a flat surface tapering out to a tiny point, we've made a tool that works well in the Moto Tool, dental drill or flexible shaft, in small jobs and restoration.

One of the most expert specialists doing hand-engraved pearl is David Nichols (Custom Pearl Inlay), and they can also supply pearl and abalone shell blanks for inlaying, the improved router bit previously mentioned, sources of engraving tools and instructions.

Our background was developed in replicating 5-string necks to made Gibson tenor banjos more useful to their new owners, as the popularity of bluegrass music grew. As our abilities became more widely known, we were asked to copy

Martin guitar inlay patterns, Epiphone, Bacon, Vega and Weymann banjo designs (to name a few of the more popular), personalized items as diverse as a white pearl Martini glass, with abalone olive and bubbles, and finally, a distinctive clear pale abalone inlay pattern, with an occasional 'colored' piece for accent, when the Morgan banjo became a reality in 1975.

In approximately 1962, a stop at John D'Angelico's luthiery shop in New York's Bowery section had yielded a nice stash of precut pearl patterns left over when a local company had gone out of business. Previous visits had produced small quantities, carefully hand-selected, and John (in frustration) offered the rest of his stock for $20.00! Back at home, the mound measured about 8 inches in diameter, and some 1½ inches deep at the center, but contained several thousand pieces of very diverse shapes. Some friends who had the first shot at sorting thru this 'nightmare' allowed the resulting psychiatry bills were likely to be much higher than our original investment!

Our goal in writing this article is simply to pass on some of our experiences to you, the reader. Our background is steeped in the 'do-it-yourself' traditions of the East Tennessee mountains, but the contacts made with woodworkers, luthiers, various suppliers, collectors and institutions, while living in the Washington, D.C. area, has given us a broad overview of the art form.

If you have a piece of oriental furniture with missing inlays, one should first carefully match the material (river mussel pearl may even be closer), and then strive for the style and workmanship of the original pieces, even if it takes quite a bit of practice or 'dry runs' to achieve this. The same analogy applies to a lot of other restoration situations, whether in muscial instruments, jewelry boxes, woodworking, etc., but we would also encourage you to be creative (and just a bit daring), with your own ideas of how inlays can be used to enhance almost anything. There is nothing quite so rewarding as having your own examples of delicately inlaid work to enjoy, and for others to admire, but there is also the liklihood that you will be storing up family heirlooms for the future.

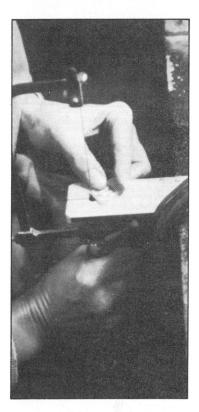

Handsawing an 'M' with the jeweler's saw.

SOURCES: (for tools, instruction, materials, precut patterns and shell blanks)

Stewart MacDonald Mfg., Inc.
Box 900
Athens, Ohio 45701
1-800-848-2273

Morgan Company
Rt. 3, Box 204
Dayton, Tennessee 37321
615-775-2996

First Quality Banjo Supply
5303 Galaxie Drive
Louisville, Kentucky 40258
502-447-5670

L to R: Mary Morgan with custom carved-top autoharp; Tom Morgan with 'mountain style' guitar; Scott Morgan with A-model mandolin.

ABOUT THE AUTHORS

Mary and Tom Morgan, with their son Scott, build and repair instruments in the Morgan Springs community on the Cumberland Plateau, near Dayton, Tennessee.

Carving Large Egg And Dart Molding

by Frederick Wilbur

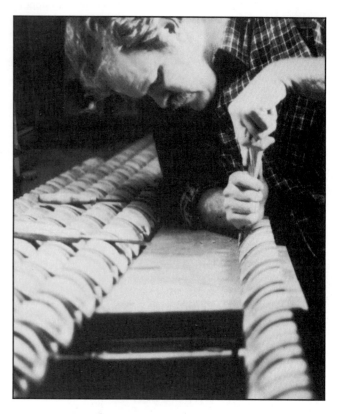

Recently, I was asked to carve fifty feet of egg and dart molding for the University of Virginia, and being an alumnus, I was happy to oblige. In fact, helping to restore one of Thomas Jefferson's architectural achievements and one of America's historic landmarks was an honor for me. The molding was a large egg and dart motif originally carved of poplar and comprised part of the cornice of a number of the pavillions along "The Lawn". Most of the moldings that I had carved were usually smaller than this 2 1/4 inch molding, and I was unprepared for the heavy-handed treatment it required. I have described some of the methods I used to tackle this job, as well as how moldings are generally done, whether a berry and sausage, acanthus leaf, or other motif.

As in most any molding, one shapes the profile of the stock first, being mindful that the final dimension of the molding may be somewhat diminished by the carving in cases of deep modeling. Also, if the carved piece fits into surrounding millwork, the ground of the carved molding should match that to which it will be applied. Originally, molding was shaped with a myriad of hand planes, but today most profiles can be manufactured efficiently by machine using standard cutters or custom ground knives. I began with a 2 1/4 inch by 2/18 inch ovolo profile supplied in mahogany by the millwork contractor. Having been furnished an original piece of the molding from one of the pavillions, I could inspect it at my leisure. I could easily appreciate the skill of the woodcrafter who carved the piece in 1820, not that he had done anything out of the ordinary, but telltale signs indicated that he had gotten the technique well in hand. He had made a scratch line with a marking gauge on the back side to mark the ground but nowhere else does there appear to be layout lines, points, etc. As to be expected, upon measurement, I found a slight inconsistency in the carving of the main elements (e.g. the borders of the eggs and the line of the dart vary), but generally the work was quite consistent. It is this mechanical consistency which makes repetitive moldings effective, and as monotonous as this may sound, there is a certain challenge in performing this sort of work. The process must be appreciated as much as the product.

Making the Pattern

I duplicated the gauge line, meant to delineate the extent of the grounding beneath the darts, but in order to keep the shape of the eggs consistent, the "V" had to be the same depth on each. I made another gauge

Ill. #1. The Pattern

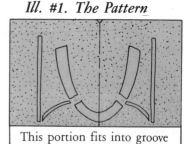

This portion fits into groove

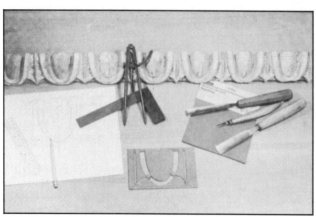

Photo 1. Only a few simple tools are needed.

Photo 2. Transferring the design.

The Profile

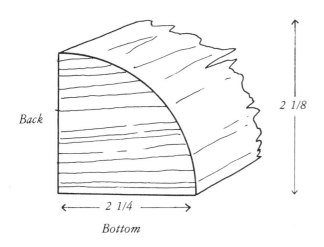

Back

2 1/8

2 1/4

Bottom

Ill. #2. Marking

Back

line for the bottom of this ''V'' (Illustration 3). I marked off the centers of the eggs with calipers. Simultaneously, I marked the eggs onto a pattern. Because I was trying to reproduce exactly the existing piece, I could make this direct transfer of measurements. I made the pattern from a thin rubber sheet. I used 1/8 inch gasket sheet available at most hardware stores or plumbing supply houses (Photo 2). Traditionally, patterns were made from thin metal sheet folded along one edge to ride on the corner of the molding. The marking of the design was done by stencil brush and thick water colors. Much of the molding I do is stained or left natural walnut or mahogany, and, as you can imagine, this method creates a bit of a mess. The use of a pencil with the thin metal sheet is difficult because the pencil rides onto the pattern instead of staying on the wood. Consequently, I have developed the use of the rubber sheet which has enough thickness to hold the pencil in place and is more versatile as it can be adapted, occasionally, to slightly different sizes and profiles. The rubber, because it will not retain a 90 degree shape, must be guided by some other device. A four inch wide and ten foot long board with a 1/8 inch groove ripped into it serves well for this purpose.

Instead of continuing to mark off the actual molding, I drew the main elements of the molding onto the pattern checking to make sure that everything was accurate and symmetrical. I nicked out a notch along the edge of the pattern where the egg centerline was in order to match it to the point I had marked with the calipers. As I worked

on the pattern I visualized which tools would fit which curves. Keep in mind that it is much better to limit the number of tools used for two reasons. First, efficiency will be served when there are only four or five tools from which to choose, and secondly, the molding turns out more crisply and less fussy. In many situations, moldings must break on corners or butt other elements in which case lengths must be determined before carving begins, and the layout must be adjusted so there is continuity throughout the joint.

After laying out the pattern on the rubber and curling it around the blank to make sure that all was well, I matched the actual tools to the curvature of the pattern and cut through the rubber onto a backing board thus creating the pattern. As I chose the tools, I noted the sequence of actions and the inherent symmetry of the design. I left several bridges at points where I thought the pattern might be weak or might shift. I inserted the pattern in the slot and clamped the molding such that the pattern curled over the molding properly. (See Photo 3). In the case of small moldings, it may be necessary to screw through the board into the back of the molding. More often than not, simple pencil lines are enough to get started as most moldings are small, and simple stabbing and cleanup suffice. On some deeply modeled moldings, it may be necessary to shade in a few repeats before carving in order to further define forms, but this is generally not necessary.

Photo 3. The pattern rides in a slot.

STARTING TO CARVE

With the large egg and dart molding, so much material had to be removed from around the egg that a number of cuts had to be performed just to define the egg location (see Photo 4). I began a few repeats on a scrap end to get the feel for the sequence and to test the accuracy of my pattern. One danger of using patterns is

Shaft of Dart   Egg   Ill. #3.

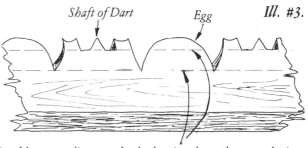

Double gauge lines on back showing how the carved piece should match the line.

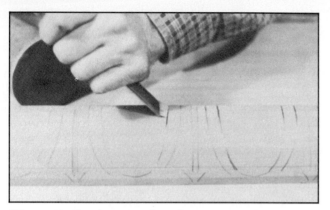

Photo. 4 Cutting egg location.

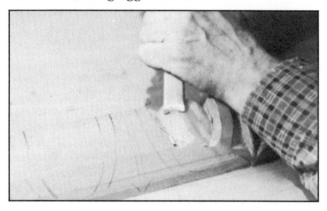

Photo 5. Shearing toward the front of the egg.

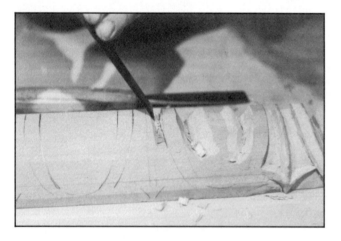

Photos 6. & 7. Cutting along the length of the shaft.

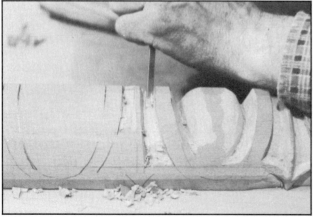

that they "creep" which explains why I marked off each unit in the beginning.

On this particular molding, the elements were quite bold and stood away from the background 1/2 inch with the "V" being 3/4 inch deep. Up close, the molding looked almost crude, but remember, that molding was thirty feet or so from the ground and required deep shadows in order to stand out.

I proceeded to chop out the "V" around the egg with a large #3 gouge. During this process, I turned the #3 over to start shaping the egg. After a few minutes working from the front side, I realized much of the time I was actually over the work and pushing my tools from back to front. Most smaller moldings are worked pretty much perpendicular to the profile, but this larger molding required more shearing cuts which, depending upon actual bench conditions, might require starting with the back of the molding facing the carver and then turning the molding around in order to complete the front. My need for efficiency resisted this double procedure, and I continued with the front of the molding towards me.

I then started work on the ten foot lengths of "blanks". Using a mallet, I walked along the length making the stabbing cuts at each "V" on one side of the egg. Then I reversed my walk and going back, stabbed on the other side of the egg. This insured an identical positioning of the tool each time. I also realized that there were two directions by which the egg was being formed. The first was the vertical chopping with the mallet to start the sides of the "V", and the second was the shearing movement toward the front in order to define the egg. (See Photo 5). After chopping out the "V" using the gouge vertically, I put the put the mallet down and sheared the sides of the wall and the round of the egg using hand pressure. The one inch #3 gouge followed the intended forms naturally and was the perfect choice for this operation.

After cutting the "V" down to the scribed baseline and forming three quarters of the egg, I turned my attention to the grounding of the darts. I proceeded to define the border of the egg's "basket" using the same #3, a 3/8 fishtail chisel at the back to start the ground, and a small skew to clean up. I used the chisel to define the straight shaft of the dart. Again, I leaned over the work in order to carve the shaft and basket about 3/4 of the way down the front. I had to be careful not to chip out the shaft as it got very thin near the outer surface, and, in fact, the last forming cuts were shear cuts along the length of the shaft (Photos 6 & 7). At this point,

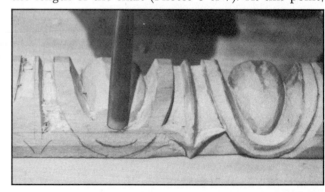

Photo 8. Working on the front of the egg.

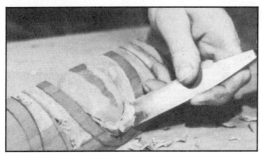

Photo 9. Cutting the basket on the front side.

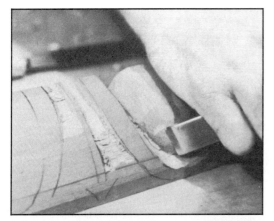

Photo 10. Completing the egg and basket.

Photo 11. Working between the dart and basket.

Photo 12. Cutting a groove along the bottom of the basket rim.

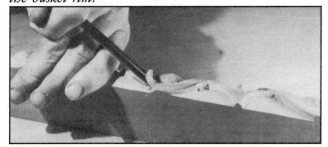

Photo 13. Cutting the top groove of the basket rim.

I checked the back to see that the eggs were the same arch two dimensionally and that the ground between baskets was the same depth.

Turning my attention to the front of the piece, I selected a #5 gouge to stab the front of the egg, lightly tapping it straight down (not perpendicularly to the profile). Then I worked around the front to meet this stop cut (Photo 8). Between the #3 and #5 gouge, I completed the egg doing both the sloping of the basket and the rounding of the egg (by turning the gouge over). On carvings this large, back-bent gouges were not necessary for the convex shaping. Note that the inner basket wall, which starts at an acute angle at the "V", flattens out to a ninety degree angle at the front of the egg (Photos 9 & 10).

Having completed the egg and the inside of the basket, I returned to the outside edge of the basket using the same #3 as in forming the egg mentioned above. I worked at defining the outside of the basket where it passes the dart curving back and where it finally meets the edge of the bottom of the molding. I made chopping cuts as before, and grounding close to the dart, I next stabbed in the curved lines which flair from the point. Slanting the #5 gouge inside and out, I created the curve and the peak in one process. This peak receded toward the ground as it neared contact with the basket, but it indeed connected with it (Photo 11). When the ground between dart and basket was complete, the molding was just about done.

The only surface modeling to be done was the groove along the basket rim, the effectiveness of the molding being dependent on clear graphic elements. The finishing cuts were made with a #7 gouge of two different widths because, as the groove neared the front edge, it became narrower as dictated by the narrowing basket rim (Photos 12 and 13).

I realized that instead of moving the entire length, I would, in fact, get involved with a short length of stock and would work down a few elements roughly and then concentrate on one before moving to another. On a smaller molding that would never happen because there just isn't that much wood to be removed. The molding in the photograph was done by walking miles up and down, stabbing and relieving, with the profile still very much in evidence. The molding was expertly installed, primed and painted afterward by the University restoration team.

Though I succeeded in reproducing the existing molding exactly, there are many variations of the egg and dart possible. In fact, the origin of the motif is not animal, but vegetable; the egg is an abstracted broad leaf and the dart is the narrower foliage squeezed between the larger leaves. (F. S. Meyer, *Handbook of Ornament*, Dover Publications, Inc., NYC 1957).

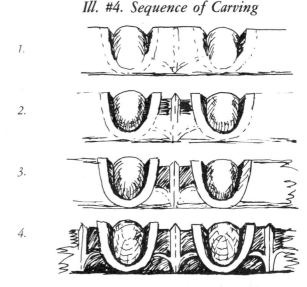

Ill. #4. Sequence of Carving

1.

2.

3.

4.

ABOUT THE AUTHOR

Frederick Wilbur is a professional woodcarver living in Lovingston, Virginia. He specializes in architectural carving and wood signs.

CUSTOM CARVED DOORS

by Connie Foss

Most of us would be satisfied to work in any well-equipped wood shop. If it were placed in a beautiful, natural setting of oak trees, that would be a bonus. The shop of Bill and Ronda Schnute goes one step beyond this. Located in Iowa City, Oak Leaves Studios is actually a forty foot covered bridge crossing a small tributary of the Iowa River.

Bill and Ronda work on a variety of projects, but their main activity is carving a series of wildlife doors. They use hardwoods of oak and walnut along with other species. The doors are highlighted with fine stained glass leaded with agate, shell, and other natural materials. A variety of animals are used as models. The river otter is shown in the photographs.

Bill began carving as a seven year old. He relies primarily on photographs and memory as a source of materials. He feels that it is not necessary to possess a talent for drawing to be a successful carver. Ronda has a masters degree in sculpture. She handles much of the firm's business transactions and her own art work, letting Bill do the carving.

Wood Preparation

Unlike many wood carvers whose wood preparation begins after going to the lumberyard, the Schnutes begin theirs at the wood lot. Having built his own electric kiln, Bill is assured that they will be using their design on quality wood dried to their own specifications. The initial cost of the wood is low or free, not counting the labor and transportation getting it to the mill. Mill costs are usually 15¢ a board foot, and costs to operate the kiln run in the neighborhood of an additional 20¢.

Information on each subject is collected from books, magazines, museum specimens, and observations of these animals.

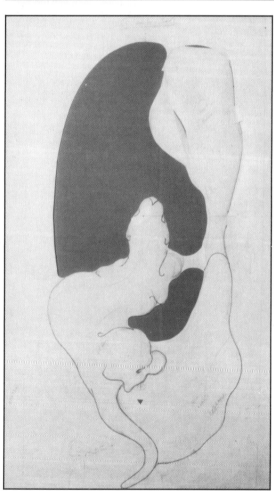

A simple line drawing developed as a pattern.

Bill feels that it is not necessary to possess a talent for drawing to be a successful carver.

Glue is applied to the edges and mating surfaces of each succeeding layer.

Though wood preparation differs according to the project, for the otter door, the next step after completing the design is to stack the wood and lay it out according to the color pattern of the wood and the straightness of the boards. For the carved panel, the Schnutes select wood that dresses to 1¾″ to 2″. Because the techniques used require edge and face gluing, all of the wood is then planed and edge jointed.

After laying out the wood, each of the three 2″ layers is clamped together and the pattern is drawn on before being band-sawed out. Bill emphasizes that before a layer is band-sawed, clamp tabs are drawn into the pattern allowing areas for the clamps for all of the edge and face gluing. Each layer has to have access for clamps so that the edges can be clamped together and beams put across the top to clamp faces together.

The most crucial part of the whole thing is to put it all together dry—a dress rehearsal—keeping in mind what it is going to do when it is lubricated with adhesive. This procedure sets all the spaces for the clamps and each layer is placed strategically around the room with its respective clamps.

The amount of time required for the final run is determined by the type of adhesive used and its relative open and closed assembly time. Adhesives that set by evaporation of the solvent, primarily yellow glues, allow only a few minutes after spreading before setting. Such a glue will not work for the marathon edge and face gluing of a Schnute project. The Schnutes have, through experimenting and research, selected a high grade industrial expoxy adhesive which allows a much more generous time frame in which to complete their myriad clampings. This glue is manufactured by Chemtech. Originally designed for boat building, it has a small degree of flexibility plus the needed strength. With an open or closed assembly time of from a half hour to a full hour, there is sufficient time for the total edge and face coating and clamping.

Bill claims that the yellow glue quality called "creep", which allows a slow movement of wood without losing the joint, is also in this state-of-the-art epoxy, coupled with a waterproof bond and a joint filling capability. The Schnutes find the use of this epoxy glue, which fills imperfections in the

An important consideration is to plan how to maintain alignment of each part when clamping pressure is applied.

It is not a matter of intense pressure but a moderate, even pressure. Waxed paper is used between glue blocks and the main panel to prevent permanent bonding.

The finished panel ready for initial rough out and shaping.

Unlike many wood carvers whose wood preparation begins after going to the lumberyard, the Schnutes begin theirs at the wood lot.

For large projects a chain saw is used for initial rough out. For smaller projects large gouges and pneumatic die grinders with carbide rotary files.

time. (A thick gob of epoxy will dry quicker because it is an exothermic chemical reaction.)

Bill cautions that a spatula or brush should be used to spread the epoxy glue for it is allergenic. "Do not use lacquer thinner to clean the epoxy from your hands for the thinner will dissolve the epoxy, and your system will absorb it. Use a commercially prepared hand cleaner that is specifically for epoxy."

After the glue sample is properly set, all clamps come off the otter project, and the carving begins.

Carving

What used to take a couple of days for rough-out can now be done in just a matter of hours with rotary files and air tools. Initial rough-out is one of the most important parts of the carving, according to Bill, for the general shape and form developed at this point will determine the quality of the carving. "You can't have a poor shape with beautiful detail and end up with a good carving," emphasizes Bill.

In addition to the air tools, Bill uses small hand grinders with dental burrs for stop cuts, claiming that using a chisel for stop cuts creates trauma in the wood by disrupting the fibers. The dental burrs will cut almost as fast as drawing a line, while a chisel is slow and tedious. Bill states emphatically, "Using modern technoogy is not diminishing the value of the final product."

Bill continues, "Only the initial roughing out of shape and form are done with the power tools; the final shape and form and all details are done with gouges and knives. All of our carvings are finished by hand. And we never sand any carvings! We like the finished wood that knives make, the ridges and all of the sharp edges. Even things like the eye balls, which are smooth surfaces in nature, are not sanded. The tiny little chip marks left by the knives break up the light and lend a softness, an aliveness. If sanded smooth, they would look flat, dead." Only the flats on the

Each prototype for a door is carved from the same species of wood the door will be produced in.

wood, superior to the more common glue and sawdust filler because it dries clear and allows the grain to show through.

After the dress rehearsal, the Schnutes are ready to mix the glue and spread it, putting the many pieces and layers together, clamping and bringing them down. Though Bill states that there are always surprises, they are minimized by this careful preparation.

For drying, the Schnutes allow approximately 24 hours, keeping a sample of the glue (poured with comparable thickness on waxed paper) to determine the proper set. The temperature of the air in the studio, in addition to the thickness, affects the setting

This short panel can now be used as the pilot on a four-spindle duplicating machine designed and built at the studio using scrap aluminum and iron bar stock.

The tenons of the top and bottom rail are cut and trimmed with routers after rough sizing with a band saw.

door are sanded to give a furniture-like finish.

The Schnutes have over 200 knives and gouges, but Bill emphasizes that the number of tools has nothing to do with the quality of the work. The quantity of tools allows a choice as to the surface texture. "If you have a number 7 half-inch wide knife, you are limited to that cut, and all of your cuts will be the same. If, however, you have a 3, 5, 7, 8, 11, you can have a wide variety of cuts and textures. An artist wouldn't paint a canvas with one color or one brush. Knives are a palette of textures," said Bill.

Straight two inch hardwood for the styles can be scarce and may not remain true with seasonal changes. Two half-thickness boards are routed to very close tolerances to fit the notched tenon. When glued together, any warpage can be eliminated.

To allow movement but prevent air infiltration, the tongue and groove which holds the panel in position is sealed with a flexible urethane foam rod.

Ample tolerances allow the panel to move freely to compensate for seasonal dimension changes. A centered steel pin at the top and bottom of the panel maintains its centered position and two to three additional pins, installed at the center of each side, center and carry the weight of the panel.

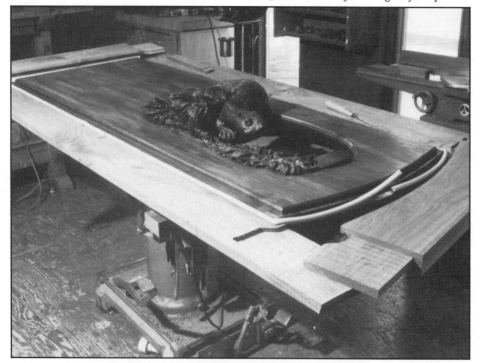

Finish

"The final step in completing a carving, applying a protective finish to the wood, usually spoils the project for me," comments Bill, who is partial to the natural color and the smooth burnished surface a sharp gouge leaves on the wood. "However, something must be done to retard the natural tendency of the wood to weather and eventually be reduced to its basic elements."

The problem is not so severe for interior work, and a penetrating oil finish or combinations of oil and urethane, with possibly one light full coat of urethane to finish, are satisfactory. Too heavy a build on carved surfaces will create a plastic look, and all sharp edges and corners will be filled in. The Schnutes prefer to use an absolutely flat varnish for the final coat.

The finish required for exterior wood is more difficult. "We have used dozens of samples of wood with different finishes on our roof in an effort to find an exterior finish which comes even close to matching the labels' claims," said Bill. Sunlight, specifically the ultraviolet wave lengths, is the main problem. The Schnutes have found that, generally, varnishes tend to be brittle and allow moisture to penetrate into the wood through small cracks, while polyurethanes, though forming a flexible surface, tend to develop a white film over time. Neither varnish or polyurethane can be guaranteed for more than six months of exposure to sunlight.

Presently, the Schnutes are experimenting with finishes which are combinations of varnish and urethanes. "The latest and best of wood technology is coming from the wooden boat building industry," states Bill.

"...knives are a palette of texture..."

The panel and inner surfaces of the grooves have been prefinished before assembly and all parts are fit together and clamped without glue to check the fit.

Moderate, uniform pressure is used to join both sides of the styles and to lock the tenons from the rail in place. Care must be taken not to allow glue to squeeze into the space between the tongue and groove of the panel which would lock the panel in place, eventually resulting in a split.

All of the procedures used on the otter door are used for the carved panels of the other doors in the series: a Great Horned Owl in oak, a Wood Duck in wild cherry, an oak tree door, an aspen and columbine door out of walnut, and, in the future, Eagle and Sea Otter doors.

A visit to the Oak Leaves Studio is an inspirational experience as well as educational. Bill and Ronda's philosophy of life and work provides a strong foundation for their creative art. These strong-willed, free-thinking young people are greatly elevating the prestige of wood sculpting.

The Finished Product

About The Author:
Connie Foss is a woodworker, writer, and carver. Her specialty is carving Arabian horses.

CROWN MOLDING INSTALLATION

by Rod Goettelmann

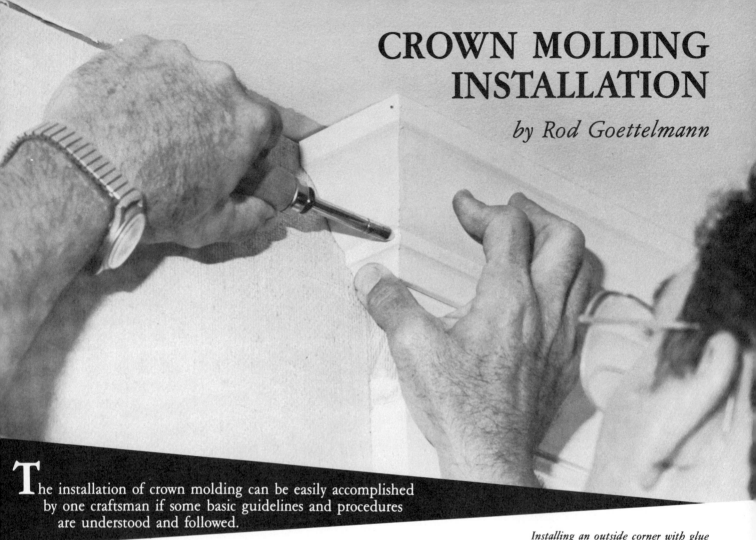

The installation of crown molding can be easily accomplished by one craftsman if some basic guidelines and procedures are understood and followed.

Installing an outside corner with glue

After the agreements with the client have been completed, the selection of the crown molding is the first major step towards a successful installation. The moldings must be clean, straight (as long as the room can accommodate) and from the same shaper run so that the cross section of the moldings is the same on all pieces. The best installation has the fewest joints possible, and moldings with a different width or profile make clean joints nearly impossible.

Prestaining or priming makes the finishing job much easier and a second coat or sanding sealer should also be applied prior to the installation unless the entire room is new trim on unfinished walls. Presanding also speeds up the entire job while controlling on-site dust which is important to a client in whose home the work is being performed. Most crown molding installations occur in finished residences and usually after the wall paper has just been hung and the ceiling painted.

The room receiving the crown molding should be empty, but if that is not possible, then all the furniture that has to remain in the room should be moved to the center and covered with clean sheets. Pictures and wall hangings should be removed on both sides of a common wall. A fine job should not be spoiled by damage to property which is why finished flooring or carpets should also be covered with clean drop cloths. The use of runners is also prudent if the weather is inclement or dirty feet are a problem.

The installation of crown molding is easier if step ladders are avoided and good work stools are used. Step ladders can mark walls or floors and they are harder to move than stools. The stools shown in the sketch are sturdy and work well for coping and other work. *(Sketch 2)*

Four inch (3 5/8") crown molding is the chosen thickness for most eight foot ceilings and three inch (2 5/8") seems to be preferred for lower ceilings. Wider crown moldings require greater saw height in the miter box, and some manufacturers do supply extension rods to raise the capacity of a miter box. *(Sketch 1)*

The second important rule for proper crown molding installation is that the molding must be placed in the mitre box at the same angle it is installed. If the angle of the molding is varied in the miter box the length of the cut is changed, so the angle must be determined and a jig used to secure that angle has to be placed in the miter box. A line is not adequate.

The angle of installation is determined by placing a piece of the molding in a builder's square so the surface flats touch both edges properly, then take the ceiling and wall dimensions which will insure that angle. *(See Sketch 3)*

The first step in the installation is to lightly mark the walls every few feet with a thin pencil line and the wall gauge which is set to the wall dimension. It is best to mark the wall because it is easier to see the mark there than if it was on the ceiling. *(See Sketch 4)* The screws can be adjusted for variations in moldings so that each job does not have to have a special gauge. The molding will cover any marks the screws might make on a painted ceiling, and the screws should be toward the finger hold so they are as far from the imperfect inside corner as possible. If a block of wood is used, the inside corner should be beveled to clear the radius left by a trowel.

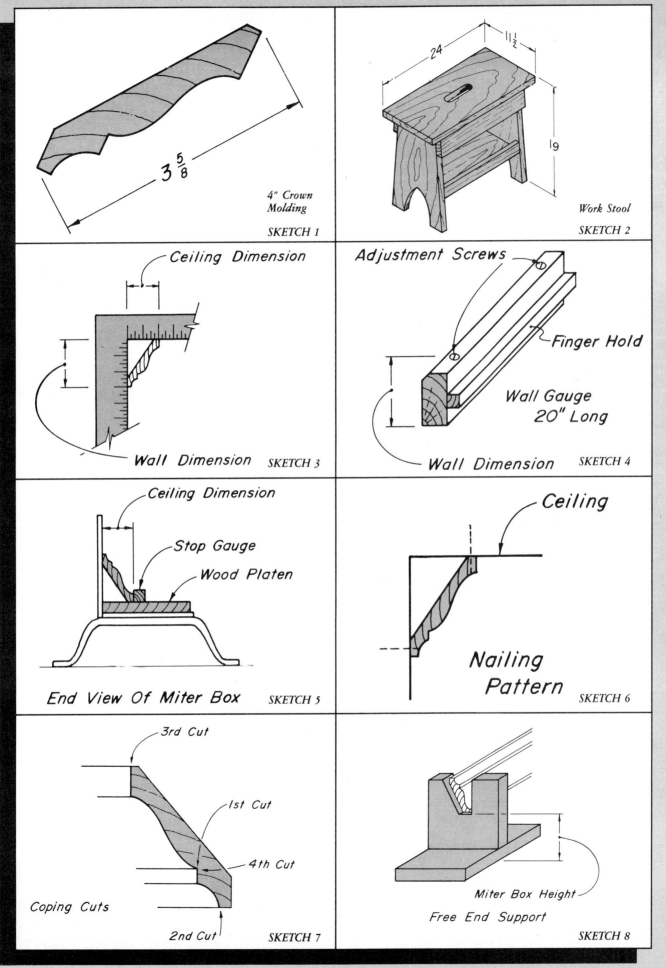

$3\frac{5}{8}$

4" Crown Molding

SKETCH 1

24   11½   19

Work Stool

SKETCH 2

Ceiling Dimension

Wall Dimension   SKETCH 3

Adjustment Screws

Finger Hold

Wall Gauge
20" Long

Wall Dimension   SKETCH 4

Ceiling Dimension

Stop Gauge

Wood Platen

End View Of Miter Box   SKETCH 5

Ceiling

Nailing
Pattern   SKETCH 6

3rd Cut

1st Cut

4th Cut

Coping Cuts

2nd Cut   SKETCH 7

Miter Box Height

Free End Support   SKETCH 8

PHOTOGRAPHS BY RICHARD MOHRFELD

A good height stool works better than a ladder

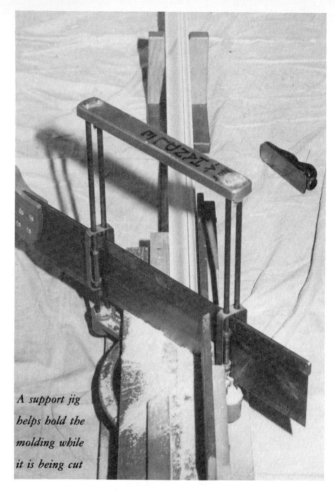

A support jig helps hold the molding while it is being cut

Using the wall gauge—Note the adjusting screens at the top

The molding is placed upside down in the miter box, and the ceiling edge is stopped by the wood strips which are fastened to a wood platen. The distance between the stop fence and the back of the miter box is the ceiling dimension. This insures that the angle when cut is the same as the angle of installation. *(See Sketch 5)*

The installer should examine the walls for defects that might indicate a poorly installed electric wire or other mechanical object. Special care should be taken in homes where non-standard work is observed or in old houses where brick nogging prevents wiring from being run in stud spaces. If a hidden object is suspected it should be marked so that nailing can avoid the area.

Use the shortest nails that will work and think of nailing crown molding as a stitching operation. The annular paneling nails seem to provide the best results, and the caution about safety glasses is to be followed.

Prestaining or priming makes the finishing job much easier and a second coat or sanding sealer should also be applied prior to the installation unless the entire room is new trim on unfinished walls.

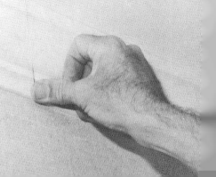

Check all lap joints before gluing and nailing

Always nail the base of the crown molding to the wall first since the gauge mark is the guide, then push the top of the crown molding against the ceiling and nail. The sketch shows that the paired nailing secures the molding even if the nails do not make a stud or ceiling joist. *(See Sketch 6)* Nailing is best on the studs and the sixteen inch interval is adequate.

The rule on joints is that outside corners are mitered and glued; while inside corners are coped. All joints along a wall are mitered and glued. Running joints are easiest if they are over a stud and at least three feet from a corner. The first piece of crown molding on a wall should be mitered back so that the second piece forming the wall joint goes over the first. It can be done the other way, but it is harder to achieve a good result. Glue is recommended, even though end grain adhesion is not as strong as edge grain, because of the long term results.

To properly mark crown molding for cutting, the installer needs to mark the bottom edge which will be up and visible when the molding is placed in the miter box. A knife mark is better than a pencil mark.

Actual installation of the crown molding starts with an inside corner. That end of the molding is a square cut and the other end is mitered for a wall joint if the molding is not long enough. If it is long enough to go from inside corner to inside corner then both ends are square cut. Full length pieces have to be measured when on an inside wall, but most cuts are marked on the molding which is better and faster than measuring.

The "helper nail" is the key to one person installation of crown molding. Prior to lifting the molding, set a nail in the wall to hold up the free end. The nail should be just above the wall mark or else the hole will show when it is removed. The free end is rested on the nail while the starting corner is adjusted and the molding is nailed in place. Always put the first nails about two feet from the end to allow some small corrections when the corner is closed. At this point the installer who uses the two stools can put them togther and walk his way down the molding as he nails. The "helper nail" has to be removed as nailing approaches the end of the first piece. The ends are nailed after the joint is made and judged satisfactory. It is easier to make a joint "work" if both ends can be adjusted.

Right handers seem to work best to the right and the opposite is probably true. This is because the hammer hand can hold the molding while the nail hand moves for nails or the nail set.

By working in one direction the mitering of marked joints becomes routine as does moving the miter box from one end of the molding pile to the other. It is best to precut one end of the molding and then mark the other end after the molding is held in place, or tacked if the installer cannot reach both ends.

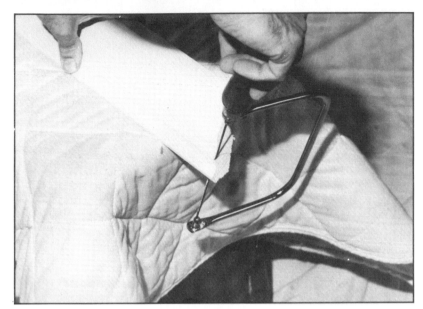

The first coping cut—The saw is slanted so that the edge is undercut

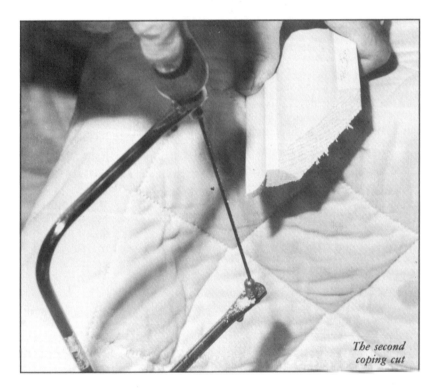

The second coping cut

The third coping cut

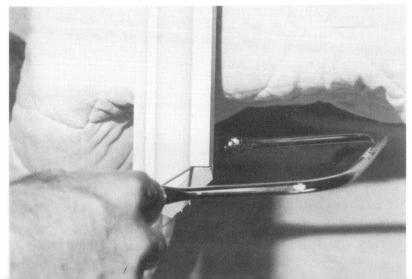

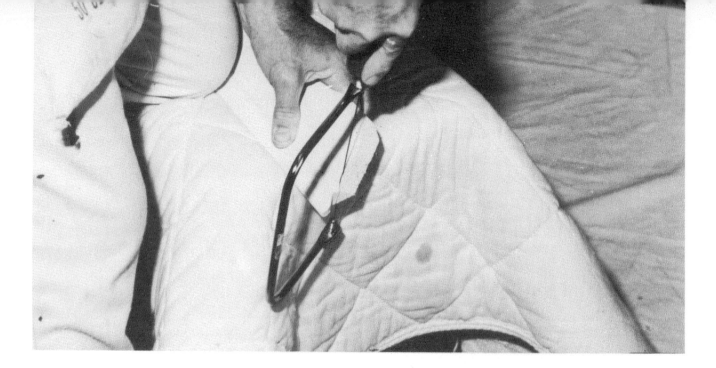

The fourth and last coping cut removes the wood

The precut for a coped joint is done on the miter box and the coping saw cut should touch the line made by the face of the molding and the miter cut. Some installers run a pencil edge over that corner to clearly show the line on unfinished wood. The best way to hold the molding for a good cut is to place it flat on top of a stool and look down on the face of the molding. This will make the coping process look natural while the four cuts are made. *(See Sketch 7)* Always under cut when coping to insure a snug fit.

A support for the free end of the moldings during cutting in the miter box is a great help as the one shown in *Sketch 8.* The bottom of the supporting notch is the same height as the bottom of the miter box.

The easiest way to do the last wall, if it doesn't end in an outside corner, is to use two pieces of molding. Both ends will be coped joints, so the first piece is coped and nailed in place with the precut lap joint already mitered back so that the second piece can be coped and checked for fit, then held in place and marked exactly for the final cut.

The wall gauge method is recommended instead of a chalk line for several reasons. Chalk is a threat to a finished room and requires nails or two people. Most ceilings are not straight and the thin pencil lines of the gauge will follow general variations of the ceiling just the same as the molding does. If there are major deflections in a ceiling, the top edge of the molding will have to be scribed to fit. The point end of the compass should be taped to prevent marks on a finished ceiling and hands should be clean for the same reason. If the ceiling or a painted wall is marked, it often is better to remove the mark by lightly sanding it with 320 grit sand paper than to use an eraser. A gum eraser is better than a pink eraser because it does not abrade wall paper or leave a colored residue.

The equipment needed for crown molding installation includes the miter box with the platen and stops, the miter box free end support, the wall marking gauge, a coping saw, a ruler, nails, hammer, nail set, nail apron, ''helper nails,'' work stools, clean tarpaulins, and crown molding. If an apprentice is part of the team then there are work stools to move and secrets for him to learn.

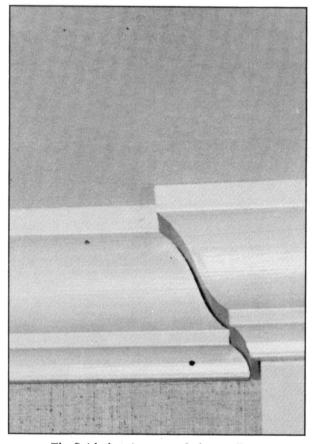

The finished coping cut ready for installation

ABOUT THE AUTHOR:

Rod Goettelmann is a cabinetmaker/builder from Vincentown, N.J.

Sam Maloof's Finish

by W. Curtis Johnson

Oil finishes have a lot of advantages. They are easy to apply. Dust is not a particular problem since the finish is in the wood and the surface is wiped dry during application. The oil brings out the beauty of the grain. The wood still looks like wood, and the smooth surface makes people want to touch it. Damage is easily repaired with some more oil and a little sanding. However, oil finishes have an important disadvantage. They just don't seem to be as durable as finishes that sit on the surface like lacquer and varnish.

I've searched long and hard for the "perfect" oil finish. I feel that people should be able to use their furniture. With tables, that means setting down glasses without fear of leaving rings. Thus, I have tested every brand of oil finish for water resistance that I could find. Most finishes are alcohol resistant because the alcohol quickly evaporates. It is the water that causes the damage.

My test is simple. After allowing the finish to cure for at least a week, I put a large drop of distilled water on the sample and let it sit until completely dry. Drying takes about eight hours. Then I wipe the spot briskly with a damp cloth, just as you might do to a table top. After waiting a day, I inspect for damage. Only a few brands show damage on casual inspection. Most brands show minor spotting when a bright light is reflected at a low angle across the surface. Of all the commercial brands that I tested, only Watco Danish Oil Finish showed no spotting at all. I added polyurethane varnish to the commercial finishes, but even these modified finishes showed slight spotting on careful inspection. In my hands, even Watco worked better as formulated than with polyurethane added.

After all the testing, Sam Maloof's finish emerged as my very favorite. It is holding up well on our coffee table and our dining room table, even though both of the tops receive constant use and are wiped off with a damp cloth almost daily.

Sam Maloof's finish isn't a secret; he has published the formula. Why don't more people use it? There are

Photo 1. The ingredients for Sam Maloof's finish: hard yellow beeswax, boiled linseed oil, gloss polyurethane, and paint thinner.

probably a number of reasons. First of all, it is not commercially available. You have to make it yourself. Perhaps Sam should get someone to manufacture the finish and market it. That would help the woodworking community as well as Sam. Secondly, the formula goes against the common lore. Tung oil is supposed to be better than linseed oil, but Sam's finish uses linseed oil. Wax is supposed to show water spots, and if you must use wax, the common lore says it should be very hard. Sam's formula uses beeswax which is relatively soft. Still, Sam is an internationally known woodworker and one of the few in the United States who makes a reasonable living at it. He has been elected a Fellow of the American Craft Council and recently received a MacArthur Fellowship, a taxfree award of $300,000 spread over the next five years. You might guess that when someone with such credentials develops a finish, it would be a good one. It is.

Sam's oil finish is really not that difficult to make. It consists of two parts: an undercoat to seal the raw wood, and an overcoat to provide extra protection. The undercoat is simply one-third gloss polyurethane, one-third paint thinner, and one-third boiled linseed oil. The linseed oil is purchased already "boiled", which is a treatment that allows it to harden more readily. The overcoat is a mixture

73

Photo 2. Sand each piece smooth using a high speed orbital sander. Begin with a coarse enough grit to remove defects and move progressively through the finer grits to 150.

Photo 3. Use a sanding block and 220 grit sandpaper to sand with the grain before applying the undercoats. Raise the grain twice with water on surfaces to receive hard use. A sanding block will acutually work quite well for all the sanding.

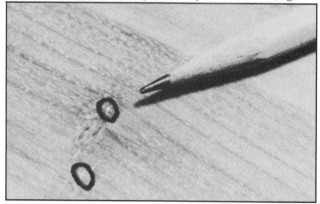

Photo 4. Check each surface carefully for defects that you may have missed. There is often a little pocket due to tear out near knots or wherever the grain reverses. They are easy to spot on a finely sanded surface since they collect sanding dust.

of about five parts boiled linseed oil to about one part beeswax. You will want the hard, yellow beeswax here. Grate the wax and add it to the oil. Warm the mixture on a stove to dissolve the wax. There is no need to make the mixture particularly hot, and it need not boil. Use the same care and common sense that you would use when heating any oil. The process is really very easy and takes only a few minutes. Let the mixture cool before using. The finish will solidify to the consistency of peanut butter.

Most readers are probably familiar with applying oil finishes. Nevertheless, I'll describe my methods in detail here for the benefit of people who are just starting out. Woodworkers can expect about half the time spent on a project to go into sanding and finishing, so relax. There is no hurrying this process if you want your furniture to look good. In general, it is much easier to make preparations for finishing before assembly. Sanding the inside of most furniture is nearly impossible. If assembly results in some dents, these are easily repaired by wetting with water for up to an hour and them sanding with 220 grit after the spot is thoroughly dry. Since my pieces are either hand planed or carefully smoothed on a planer, I can begin with 150 grit sandpaper. If your shop or skills are not yet up to planing, you will have to begin with coarser grits. First, raise any dents by soaking the spot with water. Then choose a grit that will remove the marks and defects on your pieces without undo effort. This might mean 150, 100, 80, or even the fairly coarse 60 grit. If there is really a lot of wood to remove, you may have to use a belt sander or have a local cabinet shop use their machines on your pieces before launching into the sanding described here. Don't use a vibrating sander or the old, low speed orbital sanders. They are frustratingly slow. You can sand faster by hand with a sanding block, but be sure to sand only with the grain. Even the new high speed orbital sanders are only about as fast as hand sanding, but of course they do not tire so easily. A mechanical sander is certainly not necessary, and until recently, I did all my sanding by hand.

Smooth with each grit in succession, progressing to the next finer (higher number) grit only after you have removed all the marks from the previous, coarser one. The final sanding before applying the finish is with 220 grit sandpaper. This must be done by hand with a sanding block so that the sanding is always with the grain. Shine

Photo 5. Using 400 grit wet and dry sandpaper, sand the first undercoat of thinner, polyurethane, and boiled linseed oil while wet.

a light behind the piece and check the surface carefully for defects. There is often a little tear out around knots or anywhere else the grain reverses. Sand out the defects,

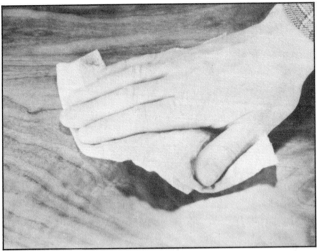

Photo 6. Wipe off <u>all</u> of the excess after the finish has soaked the surface for one half hour. After drying at least twelve hours, repeat the procedure, but use 600 grit sandpaper.

Photo 7. Apply an overcoat of beeswax and lindseed oil sparingly, and then wipe off the excess <u>thoroughly</u>. Allow the finish to dry for at least a day before repeating the procedure. All coats should be in the wood as this is not a surface finish. Applying a thick coat will weaken the finish.

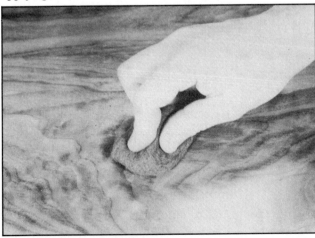

Photo 8. Buff the oil finish lightly with 0000 steel wool to give the surface a smooth feel.

but sand over a wide area so as not to create a visible pocket. A scraper (*The American Woodworker*, vol. 1, no. 3) is also convenient for this task. Most pieces will be ready for finishing when the entire surface looks good. However, surfaces that will receive hard use, such as table tops, should be wet liberally with a sponge. This will raise the grain, revealing hairlike fibers of wood. After the surface has dried thoroughly, lightly sand off the fibers with 220 grit. Repeat the process a second time. The idea is to remove the fibers now so they won't swell later when the surface gets wet, creating a visible spot on the finished furniture. Don't sand finer than 220 grit as this will only burnish the surface, closing the pores that we want to accept our oil finish.

Now you are ready to apply the first coat of undercoat. Spread it liberally over the surface and let it soak in for ten minutes. You may well have to apply a second or third coat to keep the surface wet. Then sand the surface using 400 grit wet and dry sandpaper on a sanding block. Keep the surface wet and sand with the grain, creating a mush of wood dust and finish. Allow another one half hour for the finish to soak in, and then wipe off the excess across the grain. Most wood-workers use old rags, but I find that paper towels work just fine. Wiping across the grain tends to fill the pores with the mush of wood and finish. Complete the wiping with the grain. You may feel that leaving a little extra finish on the surface will add extra protection, but don't succumb to this temptation. Wipe all surfaces completely dry at each step in this procedure. Leaving a surface slightly damp will only weaken the ultimate finish. The finish needs to be *in* the wood, not *on* it, if you don't want water spots to show. Finally, the wiping rags used in this and subsequent steps are subject to spontaneous combustion. Don't put them in a wastepaper basket or pile them in the corner. I put them in a bucket of water for a few days before disposing of them outside in a metal garbage can.

After the undercoat has dried for at least twelve hours, apply a second undercoat. Keep the surface wet for about one half hour, and then sand lightly with 600 grit wet and dry sandpaper. You don't want to sand away any more of the wood that is now sealed with undercoat than you have to. Wipe off the excess finish until the surface is completely dry. This undercoat should dry for at least twelve hours before applying the overcoats.

The overcoat of linseed oil and beeswax can be applied sparingly as it won't soak far into the undercoated wood. After rubbing on the mixture, wipe off the excess as completely as possible. With its peanut butter consistency, both applying it and removing the excess are a lot of work. To repeat the warning, if you leave a thick coat, you will weaken the finish. When the first coat has dried for a full day, apply a second coat in the same manner using light strokes with 0000 steel wool to smooth slight imperfections in the surface. Wipe off the excess and wait a few days before using the furniture.

Sam Maloof's formula ends my search for the perfect oil finish. Thanks, Sam.

About the Author

W. Curtis Johnson is a contributing editor to The American Woodworker.

Woodworking Techniques

Illustrations and text by Jerry Lyons

PRESERVING TUNG OIL

The same chemistry that allows polymerized tung oil products to harden to such a fine finish on the wood also allows larger quantities of the stuff to gel and become unusuable if exposed to air — even the small amount of air left in an only partly used container. The best way to solve this problem is simply to top up the container with water every time you use a bit of the oil. The water sinks to the bottom, the tung oil product floats discreetly on top. The two liquids do not otherwise affect each other. You can do this topping up in the original tin container, or after the first opening you can transfer the oil to a large wide-mouth glass jar (pickle jar, peanut butter jar, quart canning jar), which lets you dip your rag, sponge, brush, fingers, or whatever directly into the top of the container.

Mark H. Robbins
Milford, PA

MACHINE JOINTING END GRAIN

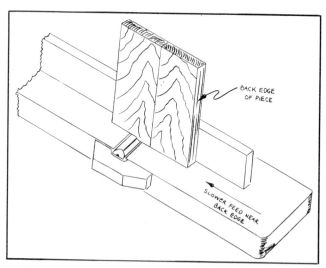

The best method I've found to joint end grain using the jointer is to size the given panel down to within 1/16 inch oversize at each end and allowing an 1/8 inch extra at the back edge. (Usually there is an edge that is not seen as much as the opposite edge or front edge.) After jointing each "end" at the allowed 1/16 inch, you may then rip or joint the back edge to remove whatever chipout that occured in the jointing process. As you're jointing, slow down the feed as you near the back edge and the chipouts will be minimal. Of course, the knife sharpness as well as how steady you handle the piece will affect the quality and accurateness of this operation. NOTE: caution should be exercised in the judgement of the smallest width pieces that should be safely jointed. Your actual width dimensions will depend on the size jointer you have available to use.

A GLUE SPREADER

A stiff plastic credit card makes a remarkably handy glue spreader. Just snake a thick line of the glue from the bottle somewhere near the middle of the areas to be glued, then spread out evenly using the card. It is a smooth, neat, quick, and clean method of spreading. To clean card after using, just flex it back and forth a few times as the dried glue will flake off. For security of your credit card, pass the card over a candle flame to remove the numbers and impressions.

Mark H. Robbins
Milford, PA

SPRAY GUN RUNS

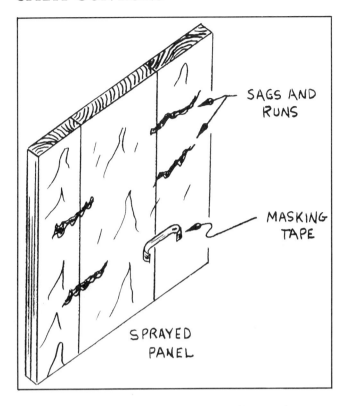

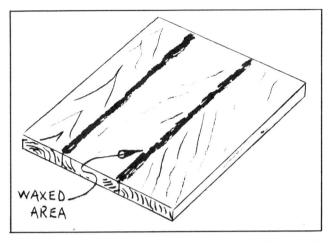

Penetrating oil finishes such as tung, linseed or Watco will dissolve the wax and sink into the wood as usual. If any wax is left behind, it may cause problems with stains and finishes such as lacquers and varnishes and removal using any clear solvent including mineral spirits will be necessary.

Mark H. Robbins
Milford, PA

EMERGENCY VISE

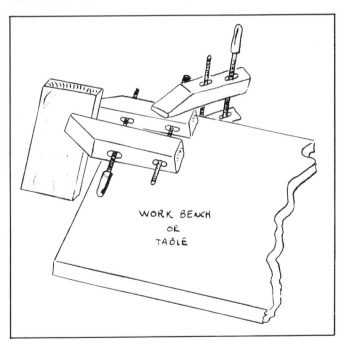

This is a trick I learned years ago while restoring automobiles. Sometimes when spray painting a panel, a run would develop. I simply get a piece of ¾ inch wide masking tape and gently put the tape over the run. The tape should be longer than the run. After gentle application with the ends of the tape loose, pull away the tape and it will lift the run right off your panel. A gentle misting from your spray gun afterwards blends everything together. All this must be done before the paint sets up and will work well on wood panels when working with lacquer type finishes.

Harry G. Sommers
Wallace, ID

WAXING

Waxing all the exposed surfaces around your joints with Butcher's wax before gluing up will save immeasurable time and labor when it comes to scraping off the dried glue that has squeezed out. With most kinds of joints, especially edge butt joints, a good time to wax is after you've got the individual pieces clamped together during your trial assembly. Be careful, however, as it is important not to slop any wax onto the glue-bearing areas. If this does occur, you may take a light pass across the jointer.

As for removing the wax, often by the time you've trimmed, cleaned, and sanded the piece, most of the wax will have been shed in one way or another. If your technique of making wide panels is to use thicker boards and then machining the glued up panel down to finished thickness in the surfacer, this operation will take care of the excess wax.

One of the most important tools a woodworker has to work with is the parallel hand screw clamps. One application for using hand screw clamps is for holding parts that might otherwise be difficult to hold in a regular vise or when a vise is not handy or available. Two of these clamps can be clamped to a sawhorse, picnic table or even a stepladder. With a little imagination, hand screw clamps can be a real asset and time-saver to the craftsman.

Robert Brightman
Great Neck, NY

Woodworking Techniques

Text by Jerry Lyons

Illustrations by Jennifer Chiles

One of the things a good craftsman must have is the basic understanding of "squaring a board". Since I have taught at the university level full time for the last twelve years, I find that many of the students that have had high school woodworking classes don't have a solid concept of the sequences that should be used in conjunction with the basic wood processing machines. These machines are the jointer, surfacer, and table saw. For several reasons too numerous to mention here, I find the students confused about the objective or reason that a particular machine was designed. That is, most people don't really understand that the only reason a jointer was designed the way it was in the first place was simply to allow you to take a rough piece of lumber and machine one of the surfaces straight and flat. Or, that you can't joint the opposite surface and expect the same piece of wood to be parrallel in thickness. A basic "six step squaring procedure" is the basis from which I teach first time woodworkers. Be sure everyone has a grasp of the terminology used to describe the six positions of a piece of wood. The illustration below describes both terminology and squaring procedure.

SIX STEP SQUARING PROCEDURE*		
Sequence	Operation	Machine
Step One	Joint Flattest Surface	Jointer
Step Two	Plane Opposite Surface	Surfacer
Step Three	Joint Straightest Edge	Jointer
Step Four	Rip Opposite Edge	Table Saw
Step Five	Crossout Best End	Table Saw
Step Six	Crossout Opposite End	Table Saw

* This is a good safe, efficient sequence of teaching people how to use the basic three wood processing machines.

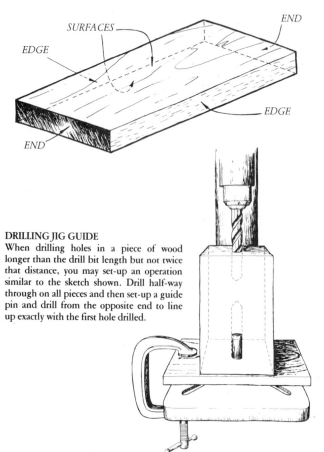

DRILLING JIG GUIDE
When drilling holes in a piece of wood longer than the drill bit length but not twice that distance, you may set-up an operation similar to the sketch shown. Drill half-way through on all pieces and then set-up a guide pin and drill from the opposite end to line up exactly with the first hole drilled.

PROPER MATCHING OF GLUE JOINTS
The sketches show the reaction of improper matching times of glue joints. The top sketch shows the edge butt glue joint right after the pieces have been clamped. If these pieces are surfaced before the glue has fully dried, a sunken joint occurs. I recommend letting the glue dry overnight, if possible. To prevent this, if the joint has been allowed to dry completely, the bottom sketch shows the levelness as it should be.

FORMING A DIAMOND MATCH IN VENEERS
To create a diamond matched pattern out of veneer, determine the finished overall sizes you need. Secure a single piece of veneer so you can layout the four smaller pieces according to the sketch below. Be very careful in preparing the joints. Use veneer tape which is a specially prepared tape made of very thin paper with lots of glue on it. The taped surface should be up after the pattern has been glued to its base material. This prevents a raised area and allows you to sand off the tape after everything is dry.

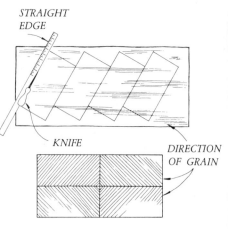

STRAIGHT EDGE

KNIFE

DIRECTION OF GRAIN

LONG HOLES
Long parts requiring a hole through the inside may be grooved, glued together and plugged at both ends so it may be placed in a lathe or for other purposes. The groove may be cut on a table saw.

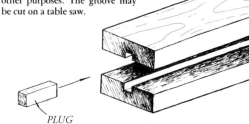

PLUG

ADJUSTABLE V-JIG
This home-made jig is used for holding round stock while cutting in flutes or reeds down a column of wood. It may be used on a shaper or perhaps a drill press using a regular fence type set-up. Once the layout marks have been drawn on one end of the wood column, the home-made brass pointer may be adjusted to accommodate the diameter to center it up. The toggle clamps hold the wood in the position necessary. This is an easy jig to make with materials already in the shop.

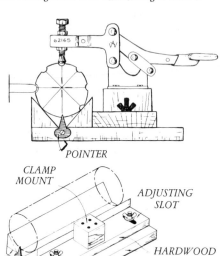

POINTER

CLAMP MOUNT

ADJUSTING SLOT

HARDWOOD

TRIANGULAR BLOCKS

The following ideas are a contribution from
KENN OBERRECHT

INSTALL A SPONGE TRAY

Most woodworkers like to keep a damp sponge nearby for wiping excess glue that seeps from joints. But the water and glue in a sponge carelessly laid aside can damage a benchtop or other surfaces. Install an inexpensive metal soap dish with screws near your workbench, and keep a sponge there, where it will always be handy, but never harmful to other objects.

FREE PAINT MIXER

Mixing water-based paints by hand is a tedius task that can be reduced to seconds by using a paint mixer in your electric drill. You can make your own mixer from a heavy-gauge wire coat hanger. Use wire cutters to cut a suitable piece of hanger and two pairs of pliers to bend the stirring end into the shape shown in the sketch. The shaft should be about 10 inches long, and the stirring end about three inches across. Remove any burrs from wire ends with a small file.

NOTE:Use only with water-based paints, as fumes from flammable substances could be ignited by sparks from the drill motor.

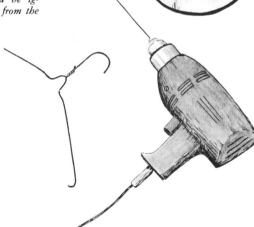

MINI CLAMPS FOR SMALL JOBS

Clamps are among the most important tools in any workshop, but most are too big for small jobs, hobby work, or clamping in tight quarters. You can make your your own miniature spring clamps from inexpensive alligator clips, available at radio and electronics outlets. Use pliers to mash the teeth of the clips flat; then make jaw cushions with small strips of vinyl tape, tightly wrapped.

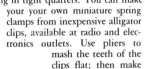

DRILLING TO PRECISE DEPTHS

In the absence of a drill press or drill-bit depth stops, you can still drill holes to predetermined depths with a fair degree of accuracy. Simply measure up the drill bit from the point and make a prominent mark with a felt-tipped pen — preferably red.

Then drill carefully and watch the mark. Simply stop drilling when the mark reaches the surface being drilled.

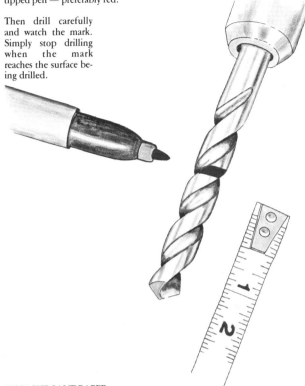

NON-SLIP SANDPAPER

No matter how much sanding you do with an electric sander or sanding block, most projects require some hand-sanding. Prevent sandpaper from slipping beneath dry, dusty fingers by first cutting sheet abrasives into quarters. Then stick two quarters back to back with strips of double-sided tape. With the abrasive on both sides, sandpaper will no longer slip your grip.

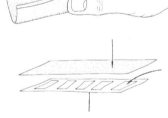

POWER-ERASE LAYOUT LINES

Most woodworking projects require layout lines for precision sawing, drilling, joining, and other operations. These lines should be removed before sanding and finishing. Cut this step to effortless seconds by using an eraser bit in your electric drill, which you can make from a plastic, tube-type eraser, available in any office-supply store. To add rigidity and eliminate wobble, cut the tube and eraser in half, and keep the extra half of the eraser as a refill.

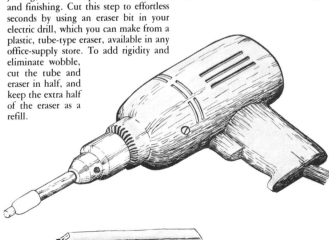

Woodworking Techniques

by Jennifer Chiles

CREATING VENEER JOINTS

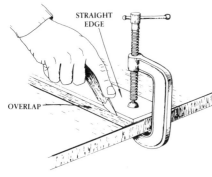

Use a super sharp X-acto knife in conjunction with a straight edge to cut the veneer straight. The species of veneer, however, will dictate whether you might want to moisten the veneer a little with a sponge. Cap the two pieces over each other and make the cut through both pieces at the same time. Remove excess and prepare for gluing.

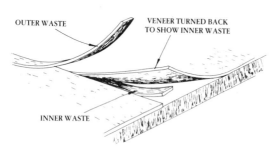

''My wife's current condition has awakened a hertofore dormant interest in making toys. Now we're talking about toys for MY BABY, not mass production, so I want to make everything myself. That doesn't mean, however, that I want to take all day. Here's a method I use for turning toy wheels quickly by reducing the time required for mounting them on the lathe. Turn a short spindle to hold the wheel blank onto a block mounted on a small faceplate. Put the wheel on the spindle, slip it into the faceplate block, and tighten the tail stock. As a fair amount of pressure is required, a ball bearing center is helpful. The spindle is small enough to let you turn the face of the wheel. If the block is smaller than the wheel blank, both edges can be rounded without reversing the wheel. A bowl gouge (this is faceplate work) ground to either a thumbnail or superflute shape should be able to shape the wheel face and round the edges without moving the tool rest. If, however, you MUST scrape, an ''L'' shaped tool rest made of 1½'' laminated plywood and a dowel post would save some time — you'd only have to move it to mount the next wheel.''

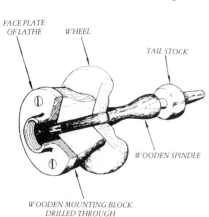

THANKS TO: DAVID R. SMITH, BALTIMORE, MD.

THREE USEFUL ADDITIONS TO THE WORK BENCH:

Here are three useful additions to the work bench. The Bench Hook is simply a flat board about 6'' x 12'', with a block fastened to each end, one on top, and one underneath. The upper block forms a stop against which work is held. It is short on the right-hand side which allows you to saw through the work without marring the bench top. The underside block rests against the front of the bench top when the hook is in use.

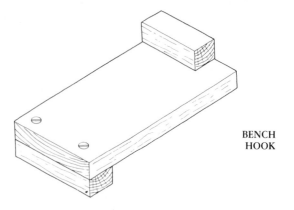

BENCH HOOK

Where the bench hook holds your work for sawing, shooting boards hold it for planing. They are especially useful when working on end grain and can be arranged for either straight or angular cuts.

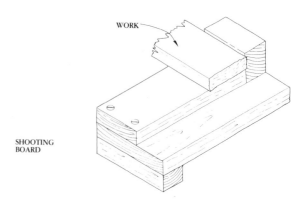

WORK

SHOOTING BOARD

One type of shooting board which is easily made, makes planing straight end grain possible without splitting off a sliver at the end of the stroke. It is a baseboard about 8'' wide and 20'' long with a 4'' board screwed on top along one edge. This forms a right-angle groove along which the plane, when laid on its side, can be slid. On one end of the top piece is a heavy block against which the work is held. The underside block rests against the front of the bench top.

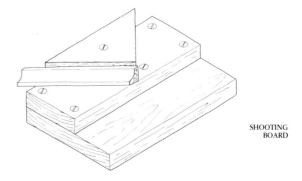

SHOOTING BOARD

Another type of shooting board is for angle planing. It consists of two pieces of wood cut to 45 degrees and screwed to a baseboard so that they form a right-angle space between them. A thicker triangular block that projects above the others is screwed into this space. The triangular block forms a surface against which the work is held. The plane is laid on its side on the baseboard and slid along the angle so that it trims the work end at a 45 degree angle. This shooting board should be held in a vice, but an underneath piece can be added so that it rests against the work bench as the bench hook does.

RESAWING

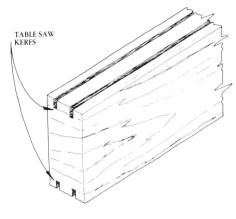

TABLE SAW KERFS

Resawing is ripping a board into thinner pieces. If you find that the resawing job is putting a lot of strain on the motor of your band saw, you might still be able to accomplish the cut if you first cut guide kerfs on the table saw. These kerfs are saw cuts on the resaw line, and they reduce the amount of material the band saw blade must cut.

GETTING A CLEAN BRUSH

Here are a couple of techniques for cleaning your brushes:

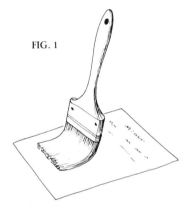

FIG. 1

Wipe the brush on newspaper to get rid of excess paint (Fig. 1). Clean your latex brushes with hot water and soap. Cleaning under a faucet is fine. Squeeze the excess paint out with your fingers or a paper towel. Use turpentine on enamel brushes. Soak an enamel brush in turpentine a short time, then press it on paper at the spot where the bristles enter the handle. This is where paint tends to accumulate, which is why we try not to dip the brush into the paint can that far. Pressing from both sides loosens it up.

After cleaning, soak your brush in the proper cleaner overnight.

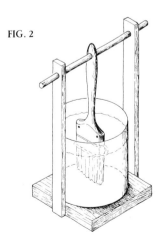

FIG. 2

I made a stand (Fig. 2) that will accommodate a wide-mouth peanut butter jar for smaller brushes, but is also large enough to hold a coffee can for larger brushes. The stand insures that a long-handled brush will still be suspended freely so that the bristles do not touch the bottom of the can and get pushed out of shape. Suspending also prevents pigment from building up and clogging the bristles. Store your brushes hanging freely; that is what the hole in the handle is for. Otherwise, the bristles can get pressed out of shape. Follow all of these steps and your good brushes will last indefinitely.

RUBBER PATTERN

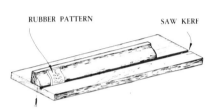

RUBBER PATTERN   SAW KERF

SCREW THROUGH JIG AND INTO BACK OF SMALL MOULDING

I carve moldings frequently and have devised a jig to aid in marking the pattern and in holding the work. This is especially convenient for working small moldings and short lengths. First obtain a 1 x 4 or 1 x 6 scrap board which is flat. Cut a saw kerf the length of it about one third of the way in from the edge. The kerf will act as a guide for the pattern. The pattern is cut from rubber gasket material 1/8 inch thick. These dimensions are not critical but the rubber should slide along the kerf. Next screw from the back into the molding which has been placed along the kerf as shown. Leave the molding screwed to the board which, because it is wider and/or longer, is easily clamped to the bench, leaving the molding clear of annoying clamps and making the carving more efficient.

THANKS TO: FREDERICK WILBUR, LOVINGSTON, VA

SPEAKER CABINET OR STAND

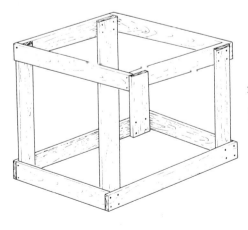

Material:
1 x 4 Pine (Frame)
1/4 Plywood (Frame Covering)

No overall dimensions are given. Build to fit your need. Normal construction techniques may be oblivious to this cabinet. If you have any problems, consult a good cabinet making book. Have fun and good luck.

THANKS TO: MICKEY FRABOTT, VALPARAISO, FLORIDA

(We know better, but sometimes we just can't help ourselves... ED.)

81

Woodworking Techniques

by Jennifer Chiles

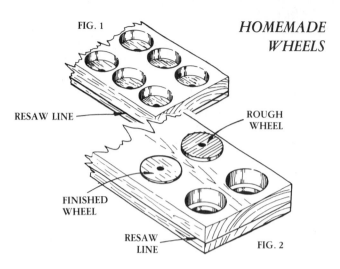

HOMEMADE WHEELS

FIG. 1

RESAW LINE

ROUGH WHEEL

FINISHED WHEEL

RESAW LINE

FIG. 2

MITER EXTENSION

Here is a way to give added control to the cross-cutting gauge on the table saw. The extension, a straight piece of wood, is counterbored for attaching with bolts or screws to the cross-cutting gauge. A kerf cut through the extension helps in lining it up with the cross-cut mark on your work. A facing of fine sandpaper provides friction to keep the work from creeping.

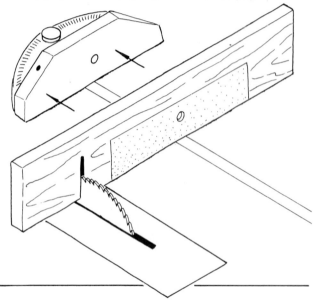

BALANCED BLADES

Many woodworkers have reconditioned older, babbit bearing equipment for use in small shops with good success. One step that is often overlooked in this reconditioning process is balancing the knives on jointers and planers. As knives are resharpened over the years, they often get considerably out of balance. This difference in weight causes premature wear and failure in the bearings. Using a beam balance, find the lighter of the knives (or lightest, if your machine has a three- or four-knife cutterhead). Center it on a knife edge and balance it end-to-end by removing metal from the back edge of the heavy end. Then, using both the beam balance and the knife edge, grind each of the other knives so as to balance them both end-to-end and with the first knife. This process can extend bearing life as much as ten-fold.

CHANGING SANDING DISCS

Stationary disc sanders are great machines, but changing the discs can be a problem. The solution lies in the fact that most adhesives used for disc sanders are thermoplastic. Blow any sanding dust off the sander to avoid contaminating exposed glue. Then, using a propane torch, heat the worn disc till the glue releases. A new disc can be stuck on immediately without adding new glue. I have changed forty or fifty discs this way without having to add glue. There is no fire hazard in this system; the metal in the backing plate absorbs and disperses the heat quite effectively. It is, in fact, impossible to ignite the glue; I tried.

*THANKS TO: MAC CAMPBELL
HARVEY STATION, NEW BRUNSWICK*

I use mostly manufactured turned parts in my toymaking; however, oftentimes a ready-made part just doesn't look right on a toy. This is especially true of wheels. A lot of my toys are made of solid cedar, so I make my own wheels in what I think is a rather novel way.

TO MAKE THE WHEELS (Fig. 1) Using a 1½'' hole saw in a drill press, I drill almost all the way through ¾'' lumber. My wheel stock lumber is 3½'' wide x 11¼'' long. This is a comfortable length to work with and one that will give me fourteen wheels. After drilling the fourteen wheels, I re-saw, taking approximately 1/8'' off the back side. The wheels fall out like pancakes.

TO MAKE THE JIG (Fig. 2) Because I use a ½'' skip tooth blade in my bandsaw, the wheels come out with a very rough side. I use a sanding jig which I devised to correct this. The jig is made of scrap lumber, ¾'' x 4'' x 10''. I made this jig by drilling ten holes with an adjustable hole cutter to almost exactly the diameter of the wheels and ½'' deep. This piece is re-sawed, leaving the back side about ¼'' thick. I drill 7/8'' holes in the back side, opposite each wheelwell. This provides a way to easily remove the wheels. I then nail together the re-sawed lumber to form the completed sanding jig. It allows me to sand ten wheels at the same time, reasonably square, on my belt sander.

THANKS TO: DON PHILLIPS, MT. PLEASANT, NC

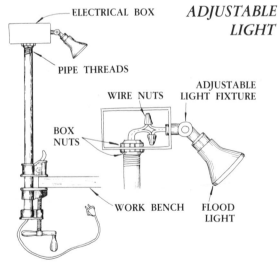

ADJUSTABLE LIGHT

ELECTRICAL BOX

PIPE THREADS

WIRE NUTS

ADJUSTABLE LIGHT FIXTURE

BOX NUTS

WORK BENCH

FLOOD LIGHT

I often carve, draw, and perform close routing at the same bench and need to readjust my lighting for each job. After being frustrated with cheap drawing lamps, I put an electrical junction box on the end of a pipe clamp and mounted swivel fixtures for flood lights on all four sides. I used a ½ inch pipe fitted with pipe clamp head and tail. Both ends must be threaded so that the tail end can be inserted into the knock-out of the electrical box; a conduit nut on either side holds the box on. Thread the supply cable through the pipe and into the box. Then attach and wire the fixture. The setup is perfect for lighting display tables or booths at craft shows because of their portability and versatility.

THANKS TO: FREDERICK WILBUR, LOVINGSTON, VA.

LUMBER RACK FOR CAR TRUNKS

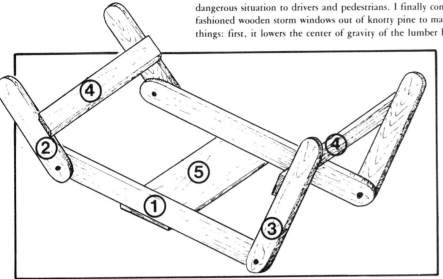

Here is an item of interest to many woodworkers—a lumber carrying rack. The best part of the rack is that it can be made from the cheapest 2 x 4's available. Since it is roughly constructed, it takes only 45 minutes or less to build. I do not own a truck and have had lumber fall out of my trunk or swing out of the passenger's window. This is a dangerous situation to drivers and pedestrians. I finally conceived the idea for a rack when I had to make 15 old-fashioned wooden storm windows out of knotty pine to match the interior of a room. Basically, the rack does two things: first, it lowers the center of gravity of the lumber by raising one end higher than the other. Secondly, it prevents any side movement of the lumber. You do not have to drive slowly because the lumber is secure.

The rack works so well that it creates a problem of overloading. Do not build the rack to take 100 2 x 4's. Thirty is a good-sized load for my mid-sized car. Vary the rack size and load to your size of car. If you can fit 4 x 8 sheets of paneling in a full-sized car, put your tool box or other weight on top inside the trunk. Wind is more of a problem than the weight with larger panels. Use elastic or rubber straps to secure the load to the rack and to hold down the trunk lid.

THANKS TO: LAWRENCE J. VITOR
HAMMOND, IN

BILL OF MATERIALS

2 ea.   2'' x 4'' x 8' lowest priced lumber
Scrap ¼'' plywood or 1'' x 3''

4 ea.   ¼'' x 3½'' nuts with bolts and washers
2 ea.   Elastic camping straps

1).   Cut to length of trunk floor, round the ends, and drill holes for bolts.

2).   Cut to height of trunk under rear window, round ends and drill holes.

3.)   Cut higher than trunk opening by at least 10'', round ends and drill holes.

4).   Cut approximately 15'', nail to number 3) at a point 1'' higher than trunk opening. Nail second piece to number 2) as low as possible. Bolt numbers 1), 2), and 3), together.

5).   Cut to size. This piece is needed for rigidity.

CUSTOM MADE SANDING DRUMS

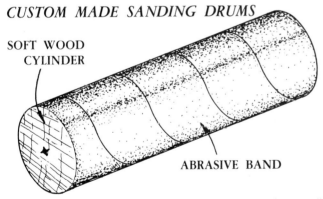

SOFT WOOD CYLINDER

ABRASIVE BAND

Occasionally a special size sanding drum is needed either to reach into a small curve in scrolls to smooth them or to sand out a concave surface. When I recently needed such a drum to be one inch in diameter and five inches long, I turned a soft wood cylinder to size, spread a generous coating of Titebond glue over it while still in the lathe, and then wrapped it spirally with one-inch wide Lightning Metalcloth aluminum oxide abrasive band available from local hardware stores or mail order tool catalogs in various grits and rolls of fifty feet. These drums do a great job because there is no break to make them bump as they cut. A No. 2 upholstery tack or thumb tack holds the band end for winding onto the drum. Another will hold the finish end, and the tacks are removed after the glue is dry a few hours later.

When using abrasive bands remember the old saying, ''The lighter you rub the better it cuts.''

THANKS TO:
CARLYLE LYNCH, BROADWAY, VA

GLUING TIPS

Here are several gluing tricks you may find useful.
I use resorcinol glue in my sign work which requires mixing with water for each glue job. More often than not, I don't use large volumes of glue each time so the routine can become a bother. I have found that using the small plastic containers which hold the frosting for refrigerated breakfast rolls makes this process a little more pleasant. I either allow the excess glue to dry (having several others to use in the meantime), after which the cake pops out, or I throw it into a bucket of water which prevents it from completely drying and is, therefore, easily cleaned. I also use acid brushes for the spreading of the glue, and at 15 cents each they are almost disposable, but I throw them into the bucket as well. About once a week I dump out the bucket and clean the plastic cups with a piece of burlap and the brushes with a wire brush and I'm ready to go for another week. I have found that using the wire brush on paint brushes occasionally is not a bad idea as well, especially for larger brushes which don't seem to get as clean as they should.

THANKS TO: FREDERICK WILBUR
LOVINGSTON, VA

Woodworking Techniques

by Jennifer Chiles

The following ideas are a contribution from FRANK PITTMAN

A QUICK SMALL CHISEL

On several occasions I have needed small special purpose chisels for inlaying or other small jobs. Rather than regrinding a regular chisel to do the job, I have been able to make some very good tools from small twist drills. You can make the handle from a short segment of 3/4" diameter dowels, shaped for a comfortable feel. Choose a twist drill of sufficient diameter. For example, I needed a chisel 1/28" wide and had a surplus of long shank 1/8" high speed steel twist drills. I simply drilled a hole in the handle with one of these bits, deep enough to cover the twist, and used epoxy glue to anchor the twist end of the bit into the handle. The twist drill shank can now be ground to any shape or width desired. The cutting edge can be sharpened like any other other chisel and these tools seem to hold a good edge.

SHANK

FLAT SANDING SURFACE

A small flat scrap of marble or granite can be converted into an excellent foundation surface for sanding small parts. Small slabs 3/4" to 1" thick are usually heavy enough to be used on a bench top without a hold down. Be sure to check the surface of the slab for flatness before using it. The one I am now using was made from a piece of an old broken marble table top. After you have found a slab, simply tape a sheet of abrasive paper to the surface and you are ready to sand.

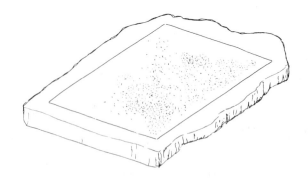

A SHARPENING AID

The strop that I use most often for the final stage in sharpening is one made from a piece of abrasive-coated leather glued to a 3/4" plywood backing. Titebond glue can be used to laminate the leather to the plywood and the assembly can be clamped together in a woodworker's vise to dry. The size of the strop is up to you. Mine is approximately 2" wide and 8" inches long. Rub the surface of the leather with some fine abrasive powder. I use 600 grit silicon carbide powder. This abrasive coating will actually cause the cutting edge to be polished.

A PADDED ROUND SANDING BLOCK

A guitar maker showed me this idea, and it has proven to be very valuable when sanding contours and curved surfaces. The block is made from a 1" dowel approximately 6" long. The foam rubber padding is actually a fairly dense foam used in making knee and elbow pads for athletes. This material is sold in roll form and is sometimes hard to obtain in small pieces. You might contact a football or basketball coach or a sporting goods shop to obtain a small piece. The foam is wrapped around the dowel and tacked or glued in place. This soft round block can make many otherwise tough sanding jobs easier.

A TAPERED ROUND SANDING BLOCK

There are many times when a round sanding block is essential when sanding scrolls and other small curves. I first saw a tool similar to this being used by a violin maker. The block can be turned from any hardwood. The one I use most is made from hard maple. The size of the tapered section can vary. Mine has a 5" long taper which is 1" diameter at the large end and 3/16" at the small end. The handle is approximately 3 1/2" long and turned to feel good in your hand. A saw kerf is made approximately 4 1/2" down the taper on a band saw. Use a V-block when doing this job. To use the block, simply insert a corner of a piece of sandpaper into the kerf and wrap it around the taper.

INSERT
SANDPAPER
HERE

RUBBER BAND CLAMPS

Large rubber bands can be used in many ways in gluing and assembly operations. The rubber band clamps that I have found most useful are those made from bicycle inner tubes. One inner tube will make two or more bands. Try to make the bands as long as possible and when smaller ones are needed, simply tie a new knot. You can make these bands by cutting out the valve stems of the inner tube and splitting the tube lengthwise with a sharp knife. Old inner tubes should be available at a bicycle shop.

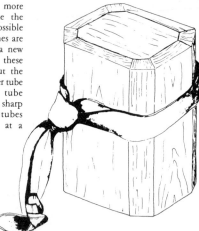

INSTALLING CABINETS

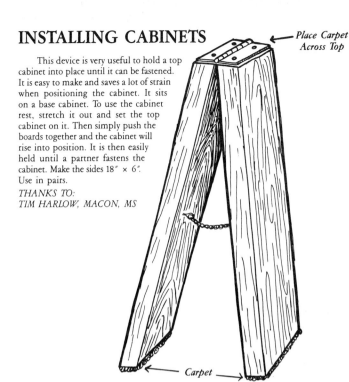

Place Carpet Across Top

This device is very useful to hold a top cabinet into place until it can be fastened. It is easy to make and saves a lot of strain when positioning the cabinet. It sits on a base cabinet. To use the cabinet rest, stretch it out and set the top cabinet on it. Then simply push the boards together and the cabinet will rise into position. It is then easily held until a partner fastens the cabinet. Make the sides 18″ × 6″. Use in pairs.

THANKS TO:
TIM HARLOW, MACON, MS

Carpet

REMOVING DENTS

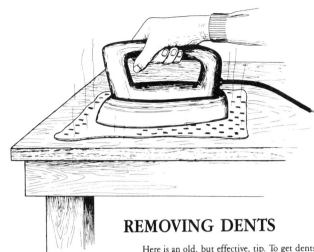

Here is an old, but effective, tip. To get dents out of wood, first wet a cloth. Hold the wet cloth on the dent and surrounding wood and press with a hot iron. As long as the cloth is moist, there is no danger of scorching the wood.

THANKS TO: TIM HARLOW, MACON, MS

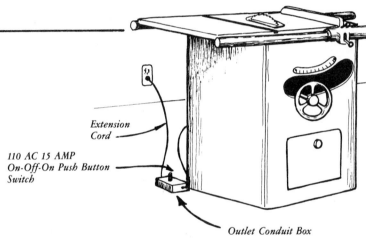

Extension Cord

110 AC 15 AMP On-Off-On Push Button Switch

Outlet Conduit Box

EMERGENCY CUT OFF SWITCH

There have probably been many times when operating a machine such as a table saw that you needed to shut the motor off in a hurry, yet were unable to remove your hands from your work. A foot operated emergency switch can be a lifesaver at such a time. The only materials required are a low profile conduit box with a duplex outlet, on-off-on switch, outlet cover, 3 wire 15′ electrical cord, and a 3 wire male plug. The total cost is around $15.00. This switch can be made for use on any number of machines.

THANKS TO: RON HOLLADAY, OXNARD, CA

BLEACHING OUT STAINS

Those black stains in oak, ash, butternut and mahogany are the result of moisture and ferrous metal reacting with tannin in the woods. It is very easy to remove these. Simply apply a solution of oxalic acid and steaming water to the entire piece, let dry, and rinse off with water. As an added note, Clorox will remove ink as well as some other stains; this also must be rinsed off.

THANKS TO: RICHARD SWIFT, HERKIMER, NY

Disfunctional Monolaminate

NEW SPEAKER DESIGN

Let the 1 × 4 legs extend all the way down to the top, thereby forming a uniformly uneven base which will conveniently not conform to any surface. Instead of using 1/4″ plywood, the cabinet is cold laminated with hot glue. The speaker may be any size, providing it fits the opening precisely and is compatible with the traditionally uneven, roughly sanded finish.

THANKS TO: RAY JANSMA, FREEMONT, MI

Speaker

1 × 4 Legs

Woodworking Techniques

by Jennifer Chiles

Woodworking Techniques would like to thank Jay Wallace of Ashland, Oregon for the tips in this issue.

WHATEVER HOLDERS

Do you ever wonder what to do with that growing pile of short lumber that is too long to throw away, but too short to do anything with? Dr. Pittman drills a large hole in the middle of square and round stock and uses them for pencils and whatever he likes to keep close at hand, but not all over his desk. They sure look better than a coffee can.

SANDER

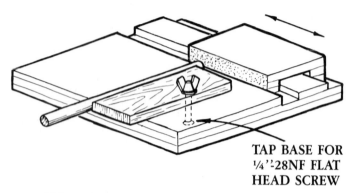

TAP BASE FOR ¼'·28NF FLAT HEAD SCREW

This tool works well for sanding the end grain on dowels. Lines are scribed on the table top for 90º and 45º positions. The block is moved back and forth in the grooves and the dowel held stationary therefore keeping the end of the dowel more accurate.

TAPERING JIG

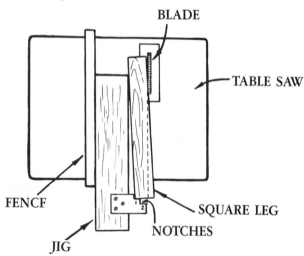

BLADE

TABLE SAW

FENCE

SQUARE LEG

NOTCHES

JIG

This jig is used for tapering a square leg. Place any side of the square stock in notch (1) of the jig. Push both the jig and the stock through the blade. Place an adjacent side of stock in the jig in notch (1) and repeat the operation. The two remaining sides should be cut in notch (2) in the same manner. It is important that the notches be exactly the same size.

CENTER LOCATER

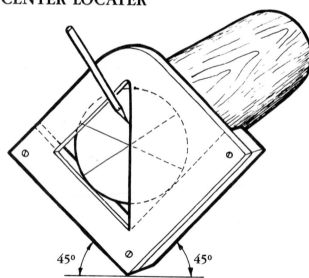

45º   45º

This tool is handy for finding the exact center of a piece of round stock. To use, rotate the round object and draw lines. Where the lines intersect is the center point of the stock. The front is plexiglass and the back is plexiglass or hard wood. The two are fused together with solvent if using plexiglass or flathead wood screws if using a wood backing. It is important to make sure that all corners are exactly 90º. This center locater can be made any size.

BANDSAW FENCE

I use my bandsaw for very accurate ripping. This fence adjusts easily by pushing in the tapered peg which locks the fence securely against the front edge of the bandsaw. A tap on the bottom of the peg releases it.

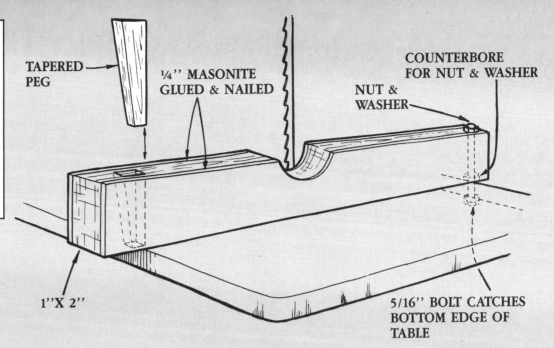

TAPERED PEG

¼'' MASONITE GLUED & NAILED

COUNTERBORE FOR NUT & WASHER

NUT & WASHER

1''X 2''

5/16'' BOLT CATCHES BOTTOM EDGE OF TABLE

NON-SLIP TOOLS

Tools for striping, drawing, and measuring are often difficult to hold with one hand.

To prevent slipping and increase ease of handling, take an old car innertube and make punchings with a paper punch. These punchings may be located to suit your needs. Secure to drafting instruments with a drop of super glue. Trim off the excess innertube from the tool at an angle. These tools can now be used for inking since they are now raised.

HANDY TOOL

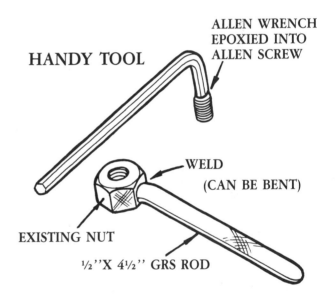

ALLEN WRENCH EPOXIED INTO ALLEN SCREW

WELD (CAN BE BENT)

EXISTING NUT

½''X 4½'' GRS ROD

I have a power tool with a table that had an underside nut which required adjusting for different operations, each time necessitating using a wrench. Welding a rod to the nut which needed frequent adjustment made the task so much easier. No longer did I need to search for the right wrench. Tighten the nut and mark to determine the best location of handle.

SEE-THROUGH TOOL HOLDER

This tool holder is just great for screwdrivers, awls, files, chisels, etc. Because of the clear plexiglass, the tools can be seen with ease. Glue dividers to masonite backing with white glue.

½'' x ½'' x 3'' DIVIDERS (RANDOM SPACING)

MOUNTING HOLE

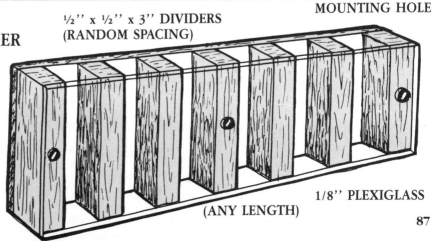

¼'' MASONITE BACKING

(ANY LENGTH)

1/8'' PLEXIGLASS

87

WOODWORKING TECHNIQUES

Text by Frank Pittman. Illustrations by Jennifer Chiles

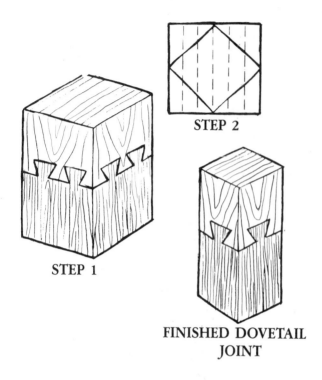

STEP 2

STEP 1

FINISHED DOVETAIL
JOINT

A TRICKY DOVETAIL JOINT

This joint has long been a woodworking conversation piece. It looks impossible but it's actually a legitimate joint. If you want to make one of these probably the easiest way is to use heavy stock to start with, say 3″ x 3″ or 4″ x 4″ material. Join the two pieces of material as shown in step one and glue them together. Next lay out a new square on the end of the stock which will cause one dovetail to appear on each surface as shown in step two. Now saw and plane away the stock to form the new, smaller square. Eureka, a tricky dovetail.

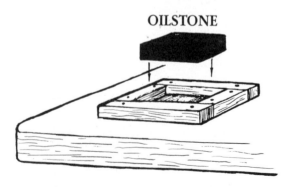

OILSTONE

AN OIL STONE RETAINER

An old technique used to prevent oil stones from being knocked off the bench is to simply attach four wooden strips to the bench top, forming a loose fitting frame for the stone. This will not only retain the stone but it will allow you to easily turn the stone for use on edge or on the reverse side.

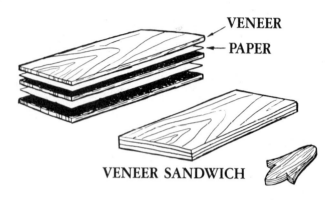

VENEER

PAPER

VENEER SANDWICH

MAKING MULTIPLE INLAY ITEMS

Inlay work frequently requires the use of items of identical size and shape. For example, a Hepplewhite bell flower pattern will require several matching veneer flowers. I produce these by first preparing a "veneer sandwich". Simply select several pieces of veneer suitable for the design and glue them together with one sheet of kraft paper between each ply. If four identical patterns are needed glue up at least five or six plies to be sure of a yield of four good pieces. After this veneer assembly has dried, at least overnight, lay out the desired shapes on the surface of the sandwich.

The items can be cut out with a precision scroll saw or a hand coping or jeweler's saw. The edges of the designs can be filed, sanded and smoothed while they are still glued together. After all shaping is complete, the individual pieces can be split from the sandwich by carefully placing a knife edge on the paper joint and slicing off sections, one at a time. The paper which remains on the surface of the inlay items actually helps strengthen the part and prevents splintering of delicate points. Inlay the pieces with the paper still on the surfaces and sand it off later.

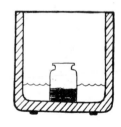

LOW
OFF — HIGH

CROCK POT

A GLUE POT IDEA

Hot animal glue is still preferred for a number of woodworking operations. One of the problems with this adhesive is the fact that it requires a glue pot. Commercially made glue pots are wonderful tools but usually cost from about $60.00 up. I've had good luck for several years using an electric "garden variety" crock pot to heat glue. You can find crock pots on sale sometimes for about $15.00. I use the pot like a double boiler, putting the glue in a small glass jar and placing it in water which is in the pot. I have also heard that some people have good luck using electric baby bottle warmers for the same purpose.

CARVING KNIVES

Luthiers often use custom made long handle carving knives in their work. I have made a number of these knives using a variety of metals for the blades. Old high speed steel jointer knives or high carbon tool steel blanks work well. Recently we have had good luck using short sections of broken power hack saw blades as the blade stock. You can usually pick up a broken blade section from a local machine shop. Shape the blade first by grinding a tang on one end like a file tang. Then make the handle to suit your hand. If you have never used a long handle knife you should give it a try. Make the handle 6½" to 7" long to start with. Later, if you don't like it simply cut it off. Glue the tang end of the blade blank into the handle using epoxy glue. Finish grinding, shaping and sharpening the blade after the handle is attached. Two of the most useful blade shapes are shown.

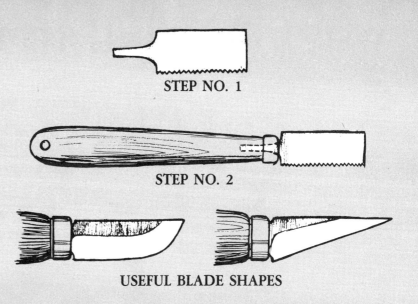

STEP NO. 1

STEP NO. 2

USEFUL BLADE SHAPES

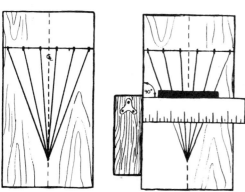
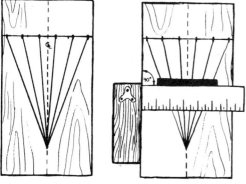

AN EQUAL DIVISION LAYOUT DEVICE

I learned this technique from a guitar maker and the concept has proven useful for a number of jobs. Guitar makers and repairmen need to be able to lay out six equal divisions for the guitar's nut. Nut lengths are not the same so a sliding scale like the one shown here works beautifully. To make this device, simply draw a line square with an edge across the blank. A small scrap of ¼" birch plywood makes a good blank. Divide this line into the number of equal divisions needed by measuring with some convenient dimension, say ½". Locate the center of the divided line and drop a perpendicular line down to a point a convenient distance away. Draw lines from this point to each of the division marks on the first line. You can now lay a square on the edge of the jig and place the part to be divided on the blade of the square and slide it up or down until you locate its length. Equal divisions can now be marked on the part.

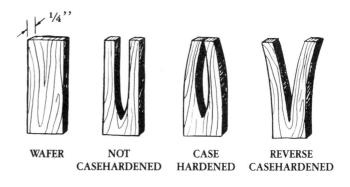

WAFER   **NOT CASEHARDENED**   **CASE HARDENED**   **REVERSE CASEHARDENED**

A RESAWING TIP

After some bad experiences with resawing a few years ago I decided to always run this simple casehardening test on my stock before resawing. Casehardening of wood refers to internal stresses which are present due to rapid drying and improper conditioning after drying. A casehardened board will look just like one which isn't casehardened. You notice the difference only when the stock is sawed or machined. If you attempt to resaw a casehardened board the wood will warp and the kerf will pinch together as you are cutting it. If you are resawing thin stock which can not be faced and surfaced to remove the warped defect the result is the production of a bunch of scrap and a wasted effort.

The test for casehardening which is used by dry kiln operators is the one I use. Simply bandsaw off a cross grain, ¼" thick wafer of wood approximately 6" in from the end of the board. Bandsaw a forked shape out of the center of the wafer. The two forked ends should remain in their original position if the board is not casehardened. If the forks pinch together or curve outward the board is casehardened and is not suitable for resawing.

ROUTER BIT STORAGE

Convenient storage of router bits can be a problem, especially as your inventory of bits increases. A simple container similar to the one shown here can help organize these important tools. The box can be made as large as you desire. Its low profile design makes it possible to keep it in a drawer comfortably. The lid is designed so the bits will be retained, side to side, thus eliminating the possibility of bits hitting each other. Each bit has its own resting place.

The box can be made by first boring a series of stopped holes, ¾" or 1" in diameter along the edge of a board approximately 1½" thick. After all holes have been bored glue a piece of 5/8" stock to the edge, covering the holes. Next, resaw the box, cutting it down the center on a band saw. Install two butt hinges for the lid and sand and finish to suit.

WOODWORKING TECHNIQUES

Text by Frank Pittman.   Illustrations by Jennifer Chiles.

DUPLICATE BRACKETS

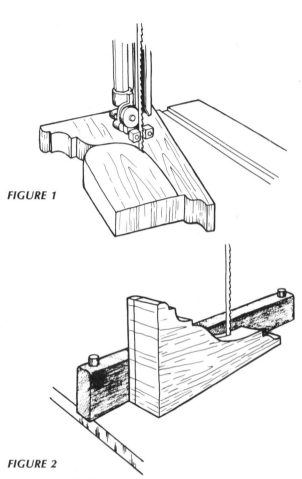

FIGURE 1

FIGURE 2

I recently added four victorian brackets to a screen door on my house. To save myself some time, I drew my pattern on a heavy piece of stock and then cut that design out on a band saw *(Fig. 1)*. I then resawed the piece, again on the band saw, into four brackets all exactly alike *(Fig. 2)*.

FILLING DENTS

To fill a depression in wood, first drill shallow holes in the depression at slightly different angles. This helps to anchor the filling. Overfill the area just a bit and allow to harden, then sand flush.

SIMPLE DOWEL JIG

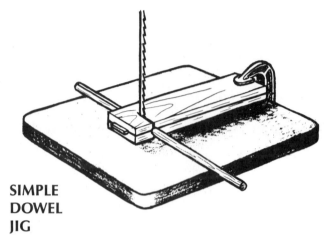

This jig is used on the band saw for cutting dowels in half to create half-round moulding. It consists of two pieces of wood that have a channel cut out for the dowel to fit into and a slot cut out for the blade. One end is clamped together and to the edge of the table, while the other end has a wedge insert to allow enough room for the dowel to be pushed through the jig.

HIDDEN NAIL

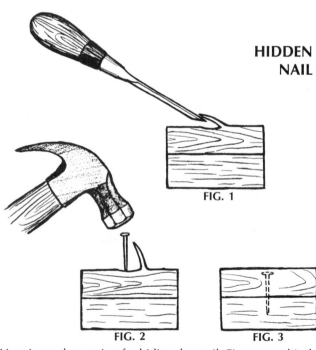

FIG. 1

FIG. 2   FIG. 3

Here is another option for hiding that nail. First use a chisel to raise a splinter of wood; don't remove the splinter, just gently bend it back as far as possible. Now drive a small nail into the depression. Finally, glue the splinter back in place and the nail is hidden.

"V" BLOCK

This block of wood with a v-cut holds a pencil for drawing lines around a circular object. Hold the pencil firmly in one hand and rotate the round object with the other hand. The height of the block can be increased by adding another block underneath.

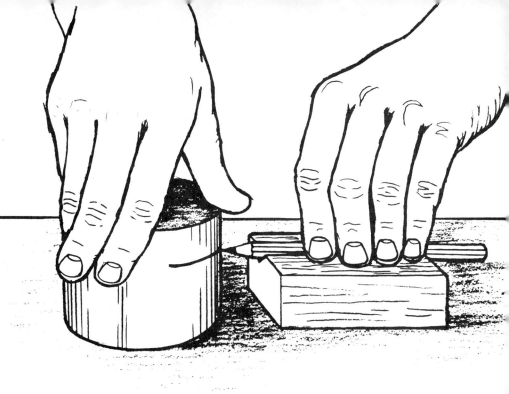

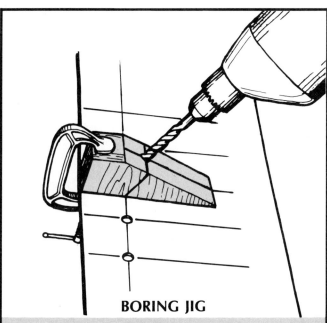

BORING JIG

This is a neat little jig to make when you have a series of holes that all need to be drilled at the same angle. Any angle can be chosen, just be sure and align the center and side lines of the jig with the center lines of the holes to be drilled in the project.

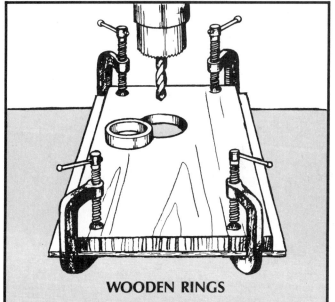

WOODEN RINGS

Next time you get the urge to make wooden rings, try this method. Clamp the wood from which you plan to cut the rings to a sheet of waste board. Drill a smaller hole with a hole-saw blade. Now replace the blade with a large one and, without moving anything, recenter the drill and cut the outer ring. You now have a wooden ring, ready to be sanded and finished.

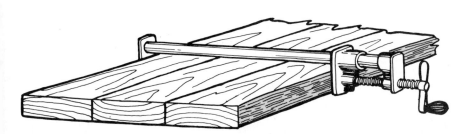

A STABLE METHOD OF CLAMPING

When gluing several pieces of stock together to form a surface such as a table top, be sure and alternate the annual rings of each piece of wood. This will prevent the table top from cupping. If possible, the stock chosen should be no wider than four inches.

WOODWORKING TECHNIQUES

Illustrations by Jennifer Chiles.

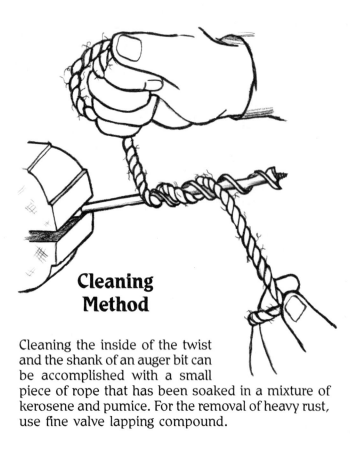

Cleaning Method

Cleaning the inside of the twist and the shank of an auger bit can be accomplished with a small piece of rope that has been soaked in a mixture of kerosene and pumice. For the removal of heavy rust, use fine valve lapping compound.

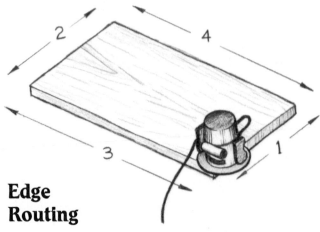

Edge Routing

When routing all four edges of a piece of stock, always route across the grain first. End grain splits easily. Most defects caused by splitting can be removed when routing with the grain.

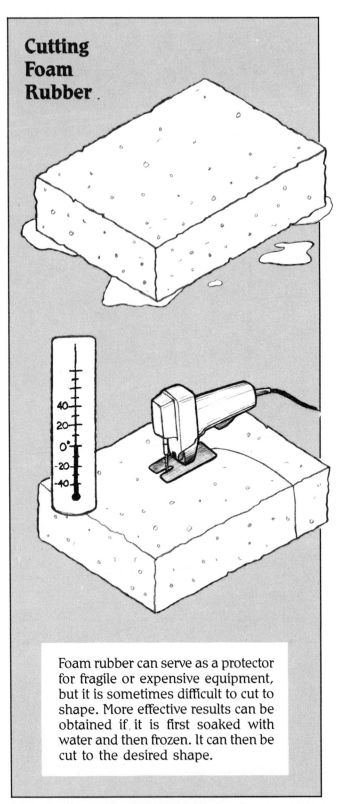

Cutting Foam Rubber

Foam rubber can serve as a protector for fragile or expensive equipment, but it is sometimes difficult to cut to shape. More effective results can be obtained if it is first soaked with water and then frozen. It can then be cut to the desired shape.

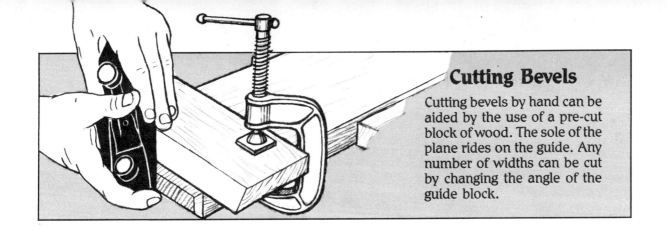

Cutting Bevels

Cutting bevels by hand can be aided by the use of a pre-cut block of wood. The sole of the plane rides on the guide. Any number of widths can be cut by changing the angle of the guide block.

Sanding Bevels

Another way of shaping bevels is accomplished by using a jig and the belt or disc sander. Bolt two pieces of hardwood to a small ¾" piece of plywood. Make sure that the angles are 45° to the sanding surface as shown. The size of the opening between the hardwood pieces will determine the size of the bevel. All four sides can be cut by simply rotating the stock.

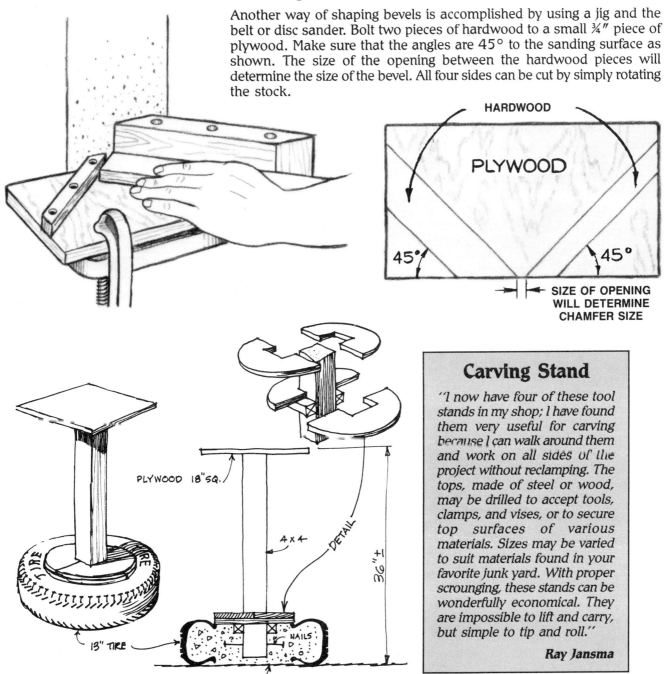

HARDWOOD

PLYWOOD

45°   45°

SIZE OF OPENING
WILL DETERMINE
CHAMFER SIZE

PLYWOOD 18" SQ.

4 X 4

DETAIL

36"±

13" TIRE

FILL WITH CONCRETE

NAILS

SECTION

Carving Stand

"I now have four of these tool stands in my shop; I have found them very useful for carving because I can walk around them and work on all sides of the project without reclamping. The tops, made of steel or wood, may be drilled to accept tools, clamps, and vises, or to secure top surfaces of various materials. Sizes may be varied to suit materials found in your favorite junk yard. With proper scrounging, these stands can be wonderfully economical. They are impossible to lift and carry, but simple to tip and roll."

Ray Jansma

WOODWORKING TECHNIQUES

Text by Christian Becksvoort

Illustrations by Jennifer Chiles

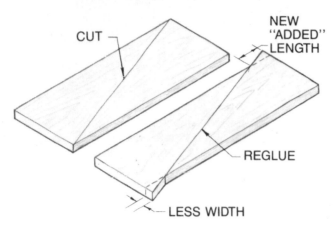

The next best idea to a board stretcher. It is possible to make boards longer if you have ample width. Cut the board diagonally, join and re-glue to desired length.

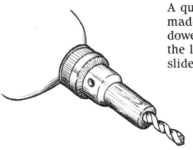

A quick depth stop can be made from a piece of dowel. Drill a hole through the length of a dowel and slide the dowel until it meets the chuck. The length of bit protruding in front of the dowel equals the depth of the holes to be drilled.

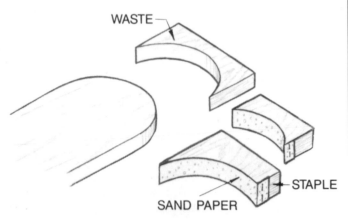

To sand curves bump free, try this: save the waste material and cut it into small pieces (about 8-9″ long), staple sandpaper along the cut edge and sand. Any irregularities produced by band sawing will be worn down. For a circular piece, one section will work all the way around. For free form curves, each section of waste is used for the corresponding section of curve.

"Speed Tenons". I used to dread making tenons: two saw set ups, hogging through 3″ of maple or cherry, and trying to hold long bed or table rails vertically against a 4″ saw fence. Speed tenons are faster, more accurate and require only one saw set up. They also produce less strain on the motor. Use a cross cutting carbide blade (carbide blades are generally safer because they produce less kick-back). Set the blade height to tenon shoulder height. Set the fence to tenon length. Now make two shoulder cuts (one on each side as with a regular tenon). Then bring the piece to the front of the blade, keeping it perpendicular to the blade at all times. Move the piece left to right and advance across the blade at the same time. Blade height is critical to tenon thickness, so try a scrap piece first. Most tenons can be cut in 15-20 passes per side, with a very smooth, very flat cheek. If you are uncomfortable free handing, use a miter fence sprayed with silicon to allow the left to right movement as you slide the wood and fence across the blade.

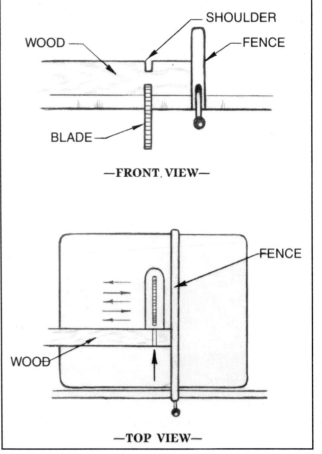

—FRONT VIEW—

—TOP VIEW—

If your table saw is too small or your miter fence will not accommodate long, wide panels (both plywood or solid) use your portable power saw. However, measuring a panel to length, measuring back from the saw blade to the edge of the saw plate and then attaching a fence is a real bother and prone to errors. To make a permanent fence, take a 12-14" strip of ¼" plywood (any desired length) and glue and/or screw on a ¾ x 4" straight fence along one edge. Run the portable power saw along that fence to cut off waste and you have a permanent fence, tailored to your saw. Now set the edge of the plywood to the exact panel length to be cut.

Making The Jig

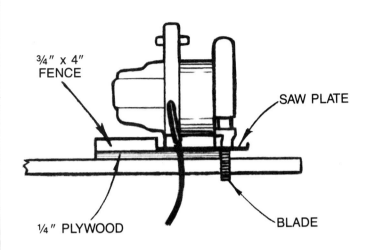

¾" x 4" FENCE

SAW PLATE

¼" PLYWOOD

BLADE

Using The Jig

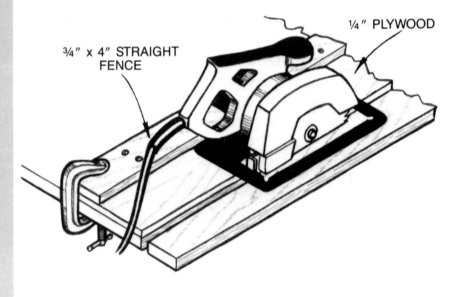

¾" x 4" STRAIGHT FENCE

¼" PLYWOOD

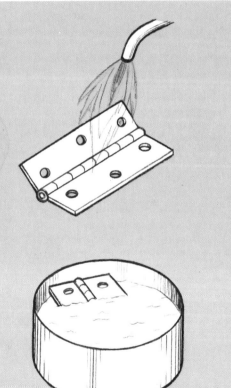

For reproduction furniture, zinc plated hinges just won't do. Use a propane torch to heat the hinge red hot. Quench in linseed oil. Cool and wipe off the excess oil. The hinge will be a bluish-gray and look like old steel.

If you are not comfortable using or sharpening a cabinet scraper, try single edge razor blades. They are sold by the box in paint or hardware stores. They are ideal for scraping small to medium surfaces, getting glue out of corners or scraping out small imperfections and they are disposable as well.

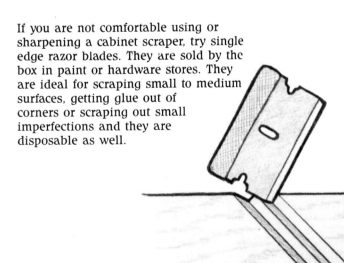

Index